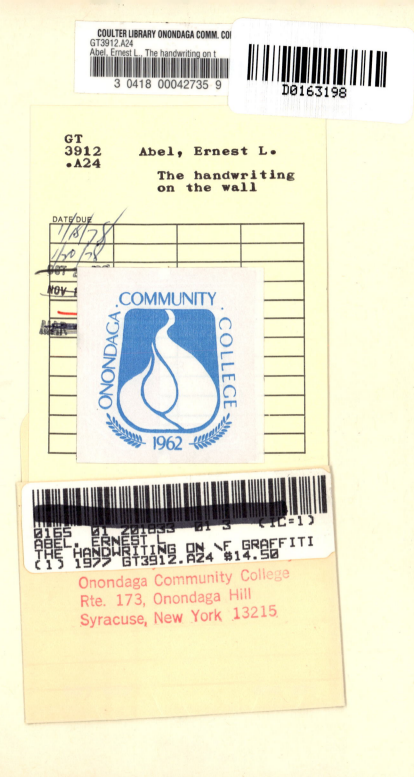

Recent Titles in **Contributions in Sociology**

Series Editor: Don Martindale

THE HANDWRITING ON THE WALL

THE HANDWRITING ON THE WALL

TOWARD A SOCIOLOGY AND PSYCHOLOGY OF GRAFFITI

ERNEST L. ABEL, *1943-*
and BARBARA E. BUCKLEY

CONTRIBUTIONS IN SOCIOLOGY, NUMBER 27

GREENWOOD PRESS
WESTPORT, CONNECTICUT • LONDON, ENGLAND

Library of Congress Cataloging in Publication Data

Abel, Ernest L 1943-
  The handwriting on the wall.

  (Contributions in sociology ; no. 27)
  Bibliography: p.
  Includes index.
  1. Graffiti. 2. Graffiti—Psychological aspects. I. Buckley, Barbara E.,
  joint author. II. Title.
GT3912.A24   301.14   76-50408
ISBN 0-8371-9475-X

Library of Congress Catalog Card Number: 76-50408
ISBN 0-8371-9475-X

First published in 1977

Greenwood Press, Inc.
51 Riverside Avenue, Westport, Connecticut 06880

Printed in the United States of America

CONTENTS

1 WHY STUDY GRAFFITI ?

What is there about an empty lavatory wall that causes people to feel the need or the compulsion to express on it their frustrations, hatreds, fantasies, desires, wit, wisdom, their innermost secrets, things they would not ordinarily reveal to their closest friends or loved ones?

One answer is that these graffiti ("little scratchings," from the Italian *graffiare,* "to scratch"; the singular is *graffito*) are a form of communication that is both personal and free of the everyday social restraints that normally prevent people from giving uninhibited reign to their thoughts. As such, these sometimes crude inscriptions offer some intriguing insights into the people who author them and into the society to which these people belong.

Of course, a serious attempt to study such fragmented and anonymous writing may be summarily dismissed by those who contend that any kind of analysis of these scribblings is an extremely arbitrary undertaking, the value of which is subjective and questionable. Admittedly, this is true—in the same way that the artifacts and inscriptions studied by archeologists are also anonymous and fragmented. Were their conclusions to be based solely on the material at hand, they too would be accused of arbitrariness and speculation. But, quite often, the archeologist is able to relate his artifacts to other sources of contemporary evidence, for example, written documents, and with such aids, he can often place his fragmented objects and inscriptions into a meaningful context with respect to the society and the events he is studying.

Noteworthy examples of these kinds of efforts are J. Lindsay's *The Writing on the Wall: An Account of Pompeii in Its Last Days,*[1] Helen H. Tanzer's *The Common People of Pompeii,*[2] and M. D'Avion's *The Women of Pompeii.*[3] These epigraphologists used the graffiti found on the walls of the city of Pompeii, which was destroyed by the eruption of Mount Vesuvius in 79 A.D., to discover what life was like in the ancient city. When these impressions were combined with eyewitness descriptions of the city and its habitants from contemporaries of this period, they were able to reconstruct a genuine record of the spontaneous life of Pompeii and the character, the private lives, and the everyday concerns of the people who inhabited its streets and homes.

Less detailed but equally valuable from a historical standpoint is the recent study of graffiti from the marketplace in ancient Athens.[4] These graffiti have been examined not only because they reveal the thoughts and petty concerns of the ancient Athenians but also because they allow archeologists to learn something about the history of writing itself. In this regard, these very early graffiti show, the archeologists at the American School of Classical Studies of Athens tell us, that "one of the earliest uses to which the art of writing was put, along with alphabetic exercises and marks of ownership, was sexual insult and obscenity."[5]

Graffiti can be traced back in history much earlier than Roman or Greek times, of course, but it was only in Greece that the common people learned to write.

Hitherto, writing had been the province of priests and nobles. When these potentates wrote anything on a wall, it reflected the thoughts, directives, or history of an elite minority. The Egyptian hieroglyphics, for example, tell us nothing about how the man on the street felt about slaving away at putting up the pyramids. The common people were without a voice until writing became "popular." When this happened, the man on the street could finally put his "beefs" down in writing.

The present study differs in many ways from those already alluded to, however, in that nearly all of the inscriptions to be discussed in this book were obtained from toilet walls rather than from the exterior sides of buildings. Graffiti appearing in such places are not a new twentieth-century phenomenon; yet inscriptions of this type either have been deliberately ignored or else have disappeared and are thus no longer available for scrutiny, except for a few examples to be mentioned shortly.

We know, for instance, that the Romans wrote graffiti, some of them obscene, upon the walls of their public latrines. Concerning these graffiti, the Roman epigrammatist Martial wrote: "Look out, I advise you, if you are anxious about being talked about, for some dark cellar drunken poet, writes his poetry on privies with coarse charcoal and stinking shit."[6]

The authorities often took measures to curb such practices. To protect their walls against such defacement, the Romans placed pictures of deities or religious emblems on their toilet walls and called down the wrath of heaven against those who were so wicked as to profane what their duty as a citizen of Rome required them to revere.[7]

The Romans were doubly concerned about this impiety. To them human waste had special significance. The Romans even worshiped gods whose primary concern was the care and protection of public latrines and the people who used them. The main deity of excrement was a goddess named Cloacina and along with the other important gods of the Eternal City like Jupiter and Juno, she too had her own temple and devotees who offered prayers in her name.[8]

We do not know whether these steps to curtail the writing of graffiti in the public latrines were very effective, but it is likely that they were taken seriously in some circles. Suetonius, the biographer of the Caesars, informs us that the authorities were very sensitive about being insulted. It was a crime, for instance, to remove one's clothing near a statue of the emperor or to carry a coin bearing his image into a latrine or a brothel. During emperor Domitian's reign (first century A.D.), this law was actually enforced, according to Suetonius, for he states that a woman was executed for undressing near the emperor's statue.[9] If the Roman authorities were prepared to back up laws such as these, it is likely that they were just as prepared to punish those who were caught defacing the latrines with graffiti, although we have no record of such punishment.

The English also had their graffiti writers. The Tower of London contains one of the most grisly collections of graffiti in all of Europe. These inscriptions were produced by kings, queens, saints, and scholars, many of them awaiting their deaths for political indiscretions or religious scruples. Mostly expressions of political or religious ideals, these graffiti were written with nails or any other hard object available at the moment. When no such instrument could be found, it was not uncommon for a prisoner to use his own blood to record his last thoughts and confessions.[10]

Thanks to the efforts of a graffitophile by the name of Hurlo Thrumbo, an anthology of eighteenth-century graffiti from the walls of London's public houses has also been preserved. Thrumbo called his anthology, which he published in 1731, *The Merry-Thought or the Glass-Window Bog-House Miscellany*. In the preface to this remarkable collection, Thrumbo declared that he had "faithfully transcribed from the Drinking-Glasses and Windows in several noted Taverns, Inns and other Public places in the Nation" various thoughts written "by persons of the first Rank and Figure in Great Britain; relating to Love, Matrimony, Drunkenness, Sobriety, Ranting, Scandal, Politics, Gaming and many other Subjects, Serious and Comical." To these he added the "Lucubrations [deep thoughts] of the Polite part of the World, written upon Walls in Bog-Houses [toilets], etc."[11]

Two examples from Thrumbo's collection have a familiar contemporary ring:

> Privies are now Receptacles of Wit
> And every Fool that hither comes to shit
> Affects to write what other Fools have writ

> You are eas'd in your Body, and pleas'd in
>   your Mind,
> That you leave both a Turd and some Verses
>   behind;
> But to me, which is worse, I can't tell, on my Word
> The reading your Verses, or smelling your Turd

Thrumbo felt that these inscriptions, many of which were scratched with diamonds, were worthy of preservation. He was dismayed at the innkeeper who kept erasing these writings from the walls "without regarding in the least the wit and learning he is obliterating, or the worthy authors," whose best thoughts are contained in these inscriptions.

It was not until 1935, however, that Allen Walker Read published, at his own expense, the first serious study of graffiti. Calling these writings folk epigraphy, Read entitled his book *Lexical Evidence from Folk Epigraphy in Western North America: A Glossarial Study of the Low Element in the English Vocabulary.*[12]

Read, who is presently a professor of English at Columbia University, states that he first became interested in graffiti in 1928 during an extended sightseeing trip through the western United States and Canada. The trip gave him ample opportunity to visit a great many public toilets. In the course of such visits, he reflects, "it was borne in upon me that these inscriptions are a form of folk-lore that should be made the subject of a scholarly study."[13] Accordingly, he copied as many of these scribblings as he had time for and since his main interest was the English language as it is used in America, he "cast the material in the form of a glossary," in the hope that "the inscriptions will be found serviceable to folk-lorists, psychologists, and sociologists" as well.[14]

In publishing this glossary, Read says that he also felt that he was making a "valuable contribution to linguistics . . . I have tapped here a written source of material that is almost solely colloquial."[15] The following excerpt is an example of how Read treated his subject matter:

> BITCH. Originally, the female of the dog family in its larger sense; but here, opprobriously, a woman. It appears largely in the phrase "son of a bitch.". . .[16]

Read then went on to show how this word was used in everyday language:

I'll kill the son of a bitch who wrote this
[*Cedar Falls, Iowa, Island Park,*
September 4, 1928]

Al Smith is a son of a bitch
[*Grants Pass, Oregon, July 21, 1928*]

Some people are poor
While others are rich
But a shit house
Poet is a Son of a Bitch
[*Ogden Utah, Artesian Park, August 16, 1928*]

Oh it is a blessing
that girls can shit without undressing
but us poor sons of a biches have
to take off our briches
[*Yosemite National Park, California,*
July 11, 1928][17]

After citing these examples, Read then summarized the various definitions of this word in sundry well-known dictionaries, in keeping with his avowed interest in the linguistic importance of these graffiti.

Since Professor Read's pioneering examination of graffiti as a serious study, there have been numerous similar studies focusing on graffiti.

In collecting examples of graffiti from public toilets, one soon becomes aware that most of the inscriptions on the walls of male lavatories have sex or biological excretion as their themes. The kinds of inscriptions typically encountered are solitary words, the overwhelming majority of which is the word *fuck*. This is followed in frequency of occurrence by single phrases such as "fuck you," drawings generally portraying genitals, and occasionally poems and longer prose passages.

The main themes found in these sexual graffiti are male and female genitalia, descriptions of heterosexual and homosexual behavior, genital, oral, and anal intercourse. The other main theme contains references to the act or the products of elimination. The latter are found either in isolation or in a context meant to express hostility toward various persons, races, religions, nationalities, institutions, and so on.

In order to appreciate fully the significance of these inscriptions we must first recognize that they are nearly always anonymous. The writers of these graffiti do not wish to be identified, in contrast to graffitists whose vandalism is confined to the outdoors. In this regard, Robert Reisner has observed that,

> as the graffiti writer gets more and more into the open areas where his chances of being seen are greater, there is a tendency for his message to be of a generalized nature without too much pornographic emphasis . . . in lavatories, or in any place where there is complete privacy, however, the messages although still often banal, are much more visceral.[18]

The writers of these "visceral" thoughts choose the toilet booth because it is a small, enclosed area where seclusion can be more or less ensured by simply locking one's self in. The narrow stall provides a world of secrecy. To be identified as the author of a graffito is to be marked with derision or pity as illustrated by these various graffiti:

Pity the man whose wisdom and wit
are inspired only
by the sweet smell of shit

The shit house poet when he dies
Should have erected in the skies
A fitting testimonial to his wit
A monument of solid shit

Man's ambition must be very small
To write his words on a shit-house wall

A thing that never should be done at all
Is to write your name on a shit-house wall
The man's a fool and he should know it
Who makes himself a shit-house poet

It is the condition of mirrors
to reflect the figure of men
and it is the vanity of
degenerates to write their names here[19]

The anonymity and the secrecy associated with writing graffiti on toilet walls suggest that there is a certain amount of shame involved in being recognized as the author of such inscriptions. "Throughout our western civilization shame is related to the uncovering of nakedness," writes H. M. Lynd. "The terms *Scham* and *schamgefuhl* in German carry implications of uncovered nudity and *Scham* is part of the compound words referring particularly to the genitals."[20]

What one society chooses to cover up, however, is often peculiar to it alone. Among certain tribes in Africa, for example, the eating of food is surrounded with great secrecy. The natives of some tribes place masks over their faces when they eat or drink, and in other tribes there is a complete prohibition against eating in the presence of others. The British anthropologist A. E. Crawley reported an incident in which the natives of the Bakari tribe were unintentionally made to feel ashamed by the actions of a German explorer. Unaware of their sensibilities regarding food, the westerner began to eat his lunch right before the eyes of these people, thereby causing them to witness an act they considered too private to be shared in public.[21]

In living among so-called primitive people and in studying their behavior, anthropologists such as Crawley have found that many of the taboos with which they surround their eating habits stem from a fear of contamination by evil spirits. From this idea there also comes the notion that the secretions and waste products that emanate from others are in some way dangerous and therefore to be avoided. By extension of this belief, any external organ that is involved in elimination or sex—the two main biological activities in which bodily substances are secreted—is also to be avoided.

It is Crawley's opinion that this widely held rule of secrecy because of fear of contamination is the basis for our present demand for privacy in activities involving the exercise of our vital functions. Further, Crawely has pointed out that the primitive human being also tends to be quite refined in his language about such functions to the extent that in some tribes it is forbidden to discuss sexual matters in the presence of a third person and to do so is regarded as a heinous sin.[22] It is as if the primitive mind looked upon the use of such language as a symbolic uncovering of the genitals, something a person would not wish to witness and something for which he might feel shame should he cause someone else to visualize such thoughts.

Although sex is no longer the topic of taboo that it once was in Western society, a certain sense of shame is still attached to the act, the discussion, or the words of sex, and deviations from sexually condoned behavior are still punishable by imprisonment in the United States. These attitudes and sentiments are typically passed on to each child by his parents during the process of growing up, and as a result the child comes to learn what kinds of behavior and language will be tolerated and what will be punished by his parents.

In studying any society, especially one's own, we are often tempted to shy away from the crudeness of its people and to emphasize instead their virtues. However, such prejudice can only lead to a rather distorted image of a society and the times one writes about. This bias was clearly appreciated by an eminent biographer of erotic literature, Herbert S. Ashbee, whose familiarity with this evasion prompted his observation that

> the poems of Martial, more especially the grosser ones, contain a vivid picture of the worst side of the private character of the Romans of the age of Domitian; and we do not hesitate to say, that the abnormal vices of a highly civilized though extraordinarily demoralized society, form an interesting and important study for the historian, moralist, or legislator, for it must be remembered that the vices of an age, not its virtues, point out most strongly the moral of that age. . . .[23]

If the art and literature of a particular culture are

often examined for insights into the preoccupations of the best minds of that society, should not graffiti be given the same consideration? Does a drawing have to be plastered on canvas or a statement printed on a page to qualify for such analysis? Do we stop searching for the inner meaning of a painting or a poem when it appears on a wall merely because we do not happen to acknowledge the wall as a suitable receptacle for art or literature? Do we stop trying to understand what motivated the artist or the writer merely because he chose to express his thoughts through some unconventional medium?

Now graffiti are certainly not art or literature in the conventional meaning of these terms. But they are expressions of someone's inner feelings, and as such they are no less a reflection of the character of a society than more polished artistic and literary works. Perhaps they are even more representative, for they are the products of the less talented segments of a society. They are not the workings of a society's best minds. But each society only has a few best minds, and they express the ideals of that society.

The everyday thoughts of the people, however, are the domain of the graffiti writer. His inscriptions give a more rounded picture of a society than is possible in the deliberately phrased message of the conventional artist or author. At the very least, graffiti helps to uncover the more elusive aspects of a society's character. Every graffito can thus be seen and/or read as a miniature autobiography of a member of a society in the sense that the graffitist reveals a part of himself and his society in all that he writes.

"No production of the human brain should be ignored, entirely disregarded, or allowed to become utterly lost," urged Ashbee, "for every writing, however trifling or insignificant it may seem, has a value for the true student, in estimating the individual who wrote it, or the period in which it was produced."[24] The very pervasiveness of graffiti over time and space, then, entitles them to serious study as much as any other record of man's civilization.

Perhaps Reginald Reynolds's forecast that graffiti will ultimately "reveal more of the truth than all the bombastic historians who will so soon be clothing our grotesque society with dignified phrases and political stercorations, representing its present antics as studied movement, to be explained in terms of high principles and rational conduct" warrants serious consideration.[25] Let us take, for example, the deliberate omission of the word *fuck* from the pages of the Webster's *New International Dictionary*. The editors state that its inclusion would have caused many people to boycott the work, and this would have defeated their main purpose.[26] Similar considerations may likewise have prompted the omission of this word and other four-letter words from other reputable dictionaries as well. But such omissions, as Ashbee clearly noted, only serve to give a partial view of what we really are and what our language really consists of.

One hundred years from now, someone chancing upon this word may wish to know its meaning. Unless the publishers of our leading dictionaries change their policy, curious readers are likely to remain ignorant of one of the most commonly used words in the English language.

Although the study of the social significance of graffiti is a rather recent phenomenon, there has been no dearth of explanations of why people write graffiti and/or what these graffiti reveal about the writers and the society to which they belong. Before we examine these theories, it is important to distinguish from the outset the two basic types of graffiti commonly encountered in our cities and towns.

The first type is what we call public graffiti. These are the initials, names, and code names that are written, carved, or spray-painted on the exteriors of buildings, trees, fences, billboards, subway cars, and so on. One historical specimen of this genre found on a tree in Tennessee was reputedly written by the famed frontiersman Daniel Boone. The graffito reads: "D. Boon Cilled A BAR in THE YEAR 1760."[27] Such graffiti are announcements of one's identity, a kind of testimonial to one's existence in a world of anonymity. They are scratched, carved, or painted onto some surface seemingly for the sole purpose of leaving one's mark. In this sense they are little different from the scent markings left by dogs when they urinate on trees, telephone poles, fire hydrants, and so on. This striving to leave one's mark via graffiti is primarily the preoccupation of adolescents belonging to the lower socioeconomic classes. Rarely are these graffiti found in middle- and upper-class neighborhoods.[28]

A completely different category of graffiti are those inscriptions that are found indoors, typically in public toilets. Alan Dundes has proposed the term *latrinalia* to designate the inscriptions that come from the toilet as against the rather loose term *graffiti*, which applies to all inscriptions, regardless of where they are found.[29]

While we share Dundes's interest in distinguishing among graffiti according to their locale, we do not feel it necessary to introduce new terms when we already have words that do the job nicely. In place of the more colorful *latrinalia*, we shall use the term *private* to refer to those graffiti found in the toilet. One reason for this preference for the public-versus-private dichotomy is that the two themes common to private graffiti—sex and excretion—represent biological activities that are so personal that they are almost always performed in relative privacy, especially in America. Likewise, the genitals are sometimes called privates to express the strength of the taboo against mentioning or observing them in public. Similarly, the toilet is often referred to as a privie to emphasize the privacy of the acts of elimination for which they have explicitly been set aside.

The motivation behind the writing of private graffiti encompasses but goes far beyond the need to leave some trace of one's existence. It is generally conceded by all those who have studied this phenomenon that the graffiti found in toilets are motivated by unconscious impulses and conflicts. It is for this reason that they tend to touch on many themes and are inherently of greater interest than public graffiti.

Read writes that "so virulent are some of these inscriptions that they are the result of nothing less than a deeply-rooted obsession."[30] While he did not elaborate on what that obsession might be, Read's general recognition of the psychodynamic significance of these writings has been echoed by many other writers. Thus W. J. Gadpaille likens graffiti to a "self-administered projective test of individuals and society."[31]

At St. Joseph's Hospital in Chicago, in fact, psychiatrists actually encourage patients to write graffiti on the walls to promote communication between patients and therapists. "These scribblings," comments the hospital's chief psychiatrist, Bernard M. Schulman, "give us diagnostic insights and clues about ways of relating to patients."[32]

Schulman hit upon this form of interaction between patient and doctor quite by accident. A schizophrenic patient who was completely uncommunicative with the hospital staff came across a blackboard and some chalk that had been left in the ward. Certain that he was not being observed, the patient secretly scribbled some words about his inner feelings. When the head nurse discovered these remarks, she wrote some questions on the blackboard and waited for the patient to discover them and possibly respond. The patient did indeed reply, and the blackboard became the medium for a dialogue.

After this initial success, other patients were encouraged to use graffiti to express their feelings. The medical staff paid close attention to these scribblings and in due course they began to perceive new ways of relating to the problems of their patients from reading what they had to say in their graffiti. From a diagnostic standpoint the graffiti also proved instructive.

For example, the psychiatrists found that manic patients tended to draw pictures rather than write, and they usually used many colors in their art work. When they did write something, they were more likely to use large letters, compared with anxious patients, who preferred small letters. Patients who preferred not to associate with others isolated their graffiti from the main body of inscriptions. Depressed patients, on the other hand, wrote very little graffiti, but when they did write something, it was usually some unhappy thought.[33]

The study of graffiti is thus not only amusing and interesting, but it may have a great deal of psychological merit in that it gives us something to think about as we try to relate graffiti messages to the human experience. This is the intriguing side of graffiti, since what may initially seem to be a trivial or coarse banality to one person may take on special significance for the linguist (for example, Read), the anthropologist (for example, Dundes), the psychiatrist (for example, Gadpaille and Schulman), and various other social scientists as they come to realize that graffiti are written by people who find the walls of our public toilets the only confessional to which they can address their thoughts and unload their troubled minds.

In the same way that archeologists and historians have been able to use graffiti to describe the daily lives and social customs of people who lived thousands of years ago, we today are able to draw upon the graffiti from our own civilization for information about ourselves, and with the aid of psychologists, anthropologists, sociologists, and so on, we can sometimes piece together our impressions concerning the meanings of these contemporary inscriptions into the kind of perspective that will hopefully shed some additional light on the preoccupations of our society.

Gadpaille, for instance, has argued that the thought patterns discernible in many graffiti may have sociological significance, since they often seem to "shed light on cultural attitudes and conflicts."[34] Likewise, M. K. Opler, professor of social psychiatry at the State University of New York at Buffalo, has stated: ". . . the plethora of crude graffiti in our society reflects our own social problems."[35] Harvey D. Lomas, a psychiatrist at the University of California's Neuropsychiatric Institute in Los Angeles, contends that "by considering the cultural milieu in which the wall writer operates, we find that the messages reflect shared attitudes and values as well as ethnocentric variations on main cultural themes."[36] Richard Freeman, a layman, has come to a similar conclusion: ". . . [these] amateur scrawls and scratchings . . . reflect the nature of the society that produce[s] them and more particularly the emotional make-up of the individual graffitists."[37]

The governors of the New School for Social Research in New York feel that graffiti are a valuable source of information concerning the mores of our society, and, accordingly, they offer a course entitled "Graffiti: Past and Present," taught by graffiti scholar Robert Reisner. Students collect examples of graffiti and then discuss their findings in class. The graffito, Reisner tells his students, "is always a sensitive barometer of change in popular preoccupations."[38] Graffiti, he emphasizes, tell us about what is happening today in our towns, cities, states, and in our own minds.

As one social commentator recently put it: ". . . the quality of our society will ultimately be judged by the quality of the graffiti on the john walls." This is not the conclusion of a professional psychologist, psychiatrist, or anthropologist. Actually, the writer of this statement is anonymous and the remark itself came from a "john" wall in Berkeley, California, circa 1970. Nor is this pronouncement unique. A graffito dialogue from a "john" wall in Chapel Hill, North Carolina, circa 1972 goes thus:

> First graffitist: If you studied the walls in
>   the restroom, you'd get a
>   great education.
> Second graffitist.   In what?
> Third graffitist: Humanity.

In *Two Thousand Years of Wall Writing* Reisner has listed two additional graffiti that encapsule this same theme:

> This wall shall be the Rosetta stone of the next civilization, consider your words well

> The only difference between graffiti and philosophy is the word fuck[39]

Although these graffiti are not typical of the material to be discussed throughout this book, they are, we believe, rather interesting if not significant in their recognition that these crude inscriptions generally reflect not only the thoughts of the people who author them but also the cultural mores and pressures that give rise to their content. True, graffiti present a vivid and often unflattering insight into the hidden side of our society; but as such they represent an intriguing, if not important, source of information for anyone—professional or amateur—who is interested in studying the behavior of human beings.

NOTES

1. J. Lindsay, *The Writing on the Wall: An Account of Pompeii in Its Last Days* (London: Mueller Company, 1960).

2. H. Helen Tanzer, *The Common People of Pompeii* (Baltimore: Johns Hopkins Press, 1939).

3. M. D'Avino, *The Women of Pompeii* (Naples: Loffredo Press, 1964).

4. American School of Classical Studies, Athens, *Graffiti in the Athenian Agora* (Princeton, N.J.: Princeton University Press, 1974).

5. Ibid., p. 4.

6. Martial, *Epigrams,* 12.61.7-10.

7. John G. Bourke, *Scatologic Rites of All Nations* (Washington, D.C.: W. H. Loudermilk & Company, 1891), p. 127.

8. Ibid.

9. Suetonius, *Domitian* (London: Penguin Books, 1963).

10. "The Tower of London," *History Today,* 1969, pp. 419-423.

11. Hurlo Thrumbo, *The Merry-Thought or, the Glass-*

Window Bog-House Miscellany (London: Privately published, 1731), p. iii. According to John Edward Gray (c. 1837), the English were considered by many to be especially prone to writing graffiti. But the French were just as likely, says Gray, to engage in such activity, provided they could not be observed doing so. In an article he published on museums around the world, he remarked: "In those places where it can be done with little chance of detection —as in the passages of the Courts of Justice in Paris—I have seen the walls much disfigured by writing in charcoal instead of chalk; the French hand in which they were written, and the names, at once showing it was the work of natives." Quoted by R. J. Walker, "Kilroy Was Here," *Hobbies,* 73 (1968), 98.

12. Allen Walker Read, *Lexical Evidence from Folk Epigraphy in Western North America: A Glossarial Study of the Low Element in the English Vocabulary* (Paris: Privately published, 1935).

13. Ibid., p. 17.

14. Ibid.

15. Ibid., p. 24.

16. Ibid., p. 37.

17. Ibid., pp. 37-38.

18. Robert Reisner, *Graffiti: Two Thousand Years of Wall Writing* (New York: Cowles Book Company, 1971), p. 4.

19. A. Jimenez, *Picardia Mexicana* (Mexico: B. Costa-Amil, 1958), p. 97.

20. H. M. Lynd, *On Shame and the Search for Identity* (New York: Harcourt Brace, 1958), p. 98.

21. A. E. Crawley, *The Mystic Rose (New York: Boni & Liveright, 1927), p. 174.

22. Ibid., p. 217.

23. Herbert S. Ashbee, *Index Librorum Prohibitorum* (London: Privately published, 1877), p. xxi, n. 20.

24. Ibid., p. xxi.

25. Reginald Reynolds, *Cleanliness and Godliness* (London: George Allen & Unwin, 1943), p. 33.

26. Ashley Montagu, *The Anatomy of Swearing* (Collier Books, 1967), pp. 304-305. However, a considerable amount

of laborious research effort has been spent delving into the origins of this word, a word that Leo Stone has called the "principal obscene word of the English language" in an article of the same title (*International Journal of Psychoanalysis*, 35 (1954), 30-56).

The word first appears in the poems of two Scottish writers, William Dunbar (1460-1513) and Sir David Lindsay (1490-1555). Its first lexographical entry occurred in 1598 in an Italian-English dictionary edited by John Florio *(Queen Anna's New World of Words, or Dictionarie of the Italian and English Tongues,* London). The most thorough analysis of its derivation is contained in a paper by A. W. Read, "An Obscene Symbol," *American Speech,* 9 (1934), 264-278. Read contends that the word does not come from the Latin *futuo,* or the Greek *phuteuo,* as argued by many of his colleagues, but rather from the German *ficken.* Its Latin cognates are *pungal* (to puncture) and *pugil* (boxer), thus giving it the connotation of an aggressive act.

27. Read, *Lexical Evidence,* p. 19.

28. H. D. Lomas and G. Weltman, "What the Walls Say Today." Paper presented at American Psychiatric Association, New Jersey, 1966, p. 6.

29. A. Dundes, "Here I Sit," *Kroeber Anthropological Society* 34 (1966), 91-105.

30. Read, *Lexical Evidence,* p. 19.

31. W. J. Gadpaille, "Graffiti: Its Psychodynamic Significance," *Sexual Behavior* 2 (1971), p. 45.

32. Quoted in "Graffiti Help Mental Patients," *Science Digest,* 41 (1974), 47.

33. Ibid.

34. Gadpaille, "Graffiti," p. 45.

35. M. K. Opler, "Graffiti Represent Thwarted Human Interests," in Gadpaille, p. 46.

36. Harvey D. Lomas, "Graffiti: Some Observations and Speculations," *Psychoanalytical Review* 68 (1973), 71-89.

37. Richard Freeman, *Graffiti* (London: Hutchinson & Company, 1966), p. 13.

38. Quoted by *Time,* November 15, 1965, p. 56.

39. Reisner, *Graffiti,* p. 42.

2 FREUD, SMEARING IMPULSES AND HUMAN CURIOSITY: THE WHYS OF GRAFFITI

More than anyone else, Sigmund Freud is responsible for increasing each individual's awareness of his innermost feelings. In spite of a tendency to overemphasize the psychosexual nature of human behavior, Freud alone alerted his contemporaries and following generations to a most complex side of behavior, one that some do not wish to acknowledge, yet one that can no longer be ignored.

Freud himself was the product of what is sometimes referred to as the Victorian era. Born in a small town in Czechoslovakia in 1856, the son of a wool merchant, Freud studied medicine at the University of Vienna and subsequently entered private practice as a psychiatrist in Vienna.

Through long years of treating neurotic patients, Freud elaborated a completely radical theory of personality development that emphasized the dynamic interplay between inborn desires and the restraints imposed by society against the expression of these desires. Through a process of self-examination that he called psychoanalysis, Freud claimed that the individual could be made aware of how the childhood resolution of the conflict between impulse and reason determines the personality of the adult.[1]

In accounting for the various different kinds of personalities, Freud contended that much of what a person does or thinks is directly due to the influence of unconscious mental processes. The unconscious, for Freud, did not mean a special region of the brain. Instead, Freud assumed that there are certain thoughts or impulses that differ from other psychic events primarily in the inability of an individual to recognize them except with the help of professional counseling. The unconscious is thus a theoretical concept Freud used to refer to causes of behavior that are not easily accounted for in terms of readily discernible factors.

Most of a person's mental activities go on beneath the level of consciousness, in the subconscious, Freud maintained, a truism that seemed clearly evident from the fact that while an individual is not conscious of most of his past at any particular moment, much of that past can be brought into consciousness without any real effort or with the help of special techniques such as hypnotism or psychoanalysis. However, there is an area of memory or mental activity that cannot be brought into consciousness at all. This is the realm of the unconscious.

Although usually inaccessible, the unconscious, Freud contended, exerts an important influence on behavior, an influence of which the individual is usually totally unaware. The reason for this blindness, he said, was that unpleasant experiences associated with the expression of certain impulses during infancy become too painful for the adult to remember. To ensure that these impulses do not reenter consciousness and thus cause painful memories, a psychic mechanism, called repression, is brought into play for the sole purpose of keeping them out. However, Freud felt that these impulses that are relegated to the unconscious had a psychic energy of their own and were constantly seeking to find some sort of release. To achieve this demand for expression they had to find some way of getting around the censor. Usually, this took the form of some disguise such as humor. Another possibility was satisfaction through vicarious substitution: Instead of hitting someone you dislike, you speak to him or about him in a way calculated to make him unhappy.

Fundamental to the theory of personality that Freud formulated on the basis of these concepts of the unconscious and the censor was the postulation of three major contributing factors to human psychic activity: the id, the ego, and the superego. According to Freud, the most important impulses that lie buried in the unconscious are the instincts everyone is born with. To emphasize their impersonal nature Freud referred to them collectively as the id (the Latin word for it).

The id is the source of all psychic energy. It represents all the biological needs that must be satisfied for life to go on, such as hunger, thirst, sleep, and so on. It was Freud's contention that two other needs or impulses are also part of the id and that they too require satisfaction. These two additional instincts are sex and aggression.

Because instincts operate at the level of the unconscious, Freud said that people are not fully aware of the influences they exert on their behavior. Because of the censor they are repressed. The only way they can eventually become known, Freud maintained, is through the long process of psychoanalysis.

Although unable to enter consciousness, the psychic energy contained in the id, Freud insisted, is constantly building up, and this build-up of energy in turn produces tension. Impulsive by nature, the id seeks to reduce this tension as soon as it begins to become uncomfortable. The various subterfuges that are eventually devised to discharge this tension will be examined shortly, but for now the main point to keep in mind is that the id is always seeking to achieve satisfaction. Freud called this inner demand for gratification the pleasure principle.

Although Freud did not identify any particular area of the brain as a pleasure zone, in 1953 James Olds discovered that such pleasure zones actually do exist in the brain.[2] In Olds's experiments, electrodes were placed in different parts of a rat's brain. The rat was then allowed to stimulate these areas electrically by pressing a lever connected to a device that delivered a very weak electrical current. To his amazement, Olds found that even when the rat was ravenously hungry and food was put into its cage, it preferred to spend all of its time pressing the lever and giving itself electrical brain shocks. This discovery thus proved that there is in fact an organic basis for Freud's idea of the pleasure principle.

Even before the discovery of pleasure zones in the brain, however, scientists had long been aware that certain instinctual drives, such as hunger and thirst, are also represented by specific areas of the brain. This is also true of the much debated sex and aggression instincts. If lesions are made in these parts of the brain, animals lose all interest in sex or aggression as the case may be.[3] Moreover, all of these areas concerned with instinctual behavior lie close together in a central part of the brain, the hypothalamus. Thus although he had no proof of the existence of an anatomical locus for the id or for pleasure, Freud was essentially correct in assuming that such areas do exist in the brain.

Similarly, although Freud was not aware of it, a French physician described a disease characterized by involuntary tic movements and coprolalia, the scientific term for uncontrollable swearing, that also tended to support the biological existence of another of Freud's hypothetical mechanisms—the censor. People who suffer from the foul-mouth disease or the cursing disease, as this disorder has come to be called (also called Tourette's syndrome after Georges Gilles de la Tourette, the French physician who described it in 1885), are simply unable to hold back the expression of obscenities. They cannot control what they say or when they say it, and they utter such streams of obscenities that they are forced to run off by themselves so that their foul language will no longer be imposed on the unsuspecting.[4]

Recently, a letter published in the journal of the American Medical Association (April 29, 1974) called attention to a case of Tourette's syndrome at Georgetown University and suggested that it had been the basis for the nightmarish novel *The Exorcist*. Anyone who read that book or saw the movie will instantly appreciate the horrible nature of this disorder.

At first medical researchers were baffled by this bizarre behavior. One mother of a young boy suffering from Tourette's disease recalls that her son began swearing uncontrollably when he was only four years old. By the time he was five, he was uttering lists of obscenities.

Initially, psychiatrists believed that the swearing syndrome was caused by psychological factors. Today, a drug called haloperidol has been used successfully to control the symptoms of Tourette's disease, and because the disorder is so responsive to drug treatment, researchers believe that the uncontrollable swearing is due to some physiological rather than psychological factor. One of the side effects of this drug, however, is a marked decrease in libido. Patients who take haloperidol exhibit little interest in the opposite sex. Soon after they stop taking the drug, their libido returns. On the basis of its dual action on coprolalia and the sex drive, it is possible that the drug may thus be affecting a part of the brain that controls or restrains the expression of human passions whether they be physical or verbal. In other words, there may in fact be a real censor mechanism in the human brain that controls what we say and do, just as Freud suggested more than 50 years ago.

The existence of such a censor mechanism gives rise to a whole series of intriguing possibilities. Are some people born with a more highly developed or strait-laced censor than others? Some people are born more intelligent than others. Some people have a greater capacity to learn than others. What if the censor mechanism is hereditary in the same way that intelligence is hereditary? What if, as Carl Gustav Jung suggested, a person is born with a collective unconscious (present in everyone and consisting of a predetermined inborn predisposition to respond to the environment in a certain way)? Perhaps there is an *archetype*, Jung's term for a particular predisposition that is derived from human beings' ancestral past, that goes back to a time when people viewed sex and excretions in an entirely different light from today. In a remarkable book entitled *Scatological Rites of all Nations*, John G. Bourke has in fact shown that human excretions were at one time endowed with special religious and magical significance.[6] At one time, and in some primitive societies, it was not uncommon to eat feces or drink urine as part of a religious ceremony, and such practices are still common. As civilization evolved and people's ideas about their waste matter changed, society began to view such practices in an entirely different light, one that was more restrictive rather than accepting of such behavior. Eventually, the average person no longer engaged in such activities, but nevertheless, the special socioreligious significance of his waste remained a part of his collective unconscious. Because of their former religious associations, feces and urine were not to be treated profanely. To ensure that this would not occur the censor mechanism evolved. A similar pattern of development resulted in sexual behavior being invested with special significance.

While an anatomical basis for the instinctual side of the human being's nature has been located and evidence exists for a censorship mechanism as well, the other two components of personality postulated by Freud—the ego and superego—still exist only as concepts, not fact. But before we discuss the second component, the ego, let us examine the concept of the superego.

According to Freud, the superego represents the internalization of all those precepts imposed upon the individual by parents, teachers, and so on. In the course of socialization, these authorities instill in the child those social standards that they themselves endorse. These standards become imprinted upon the child and act as a barrier against the expression of the id. This barrier, which Freud called the superego, is synonymous with what is generally referred to as the conscience. It is the superego's task to inhibit the free expression of the id, especially when it seeks an outlet for its pent-up sexual and aggressive energy, since these are the instincts most carefully controlled by society.

As a result of the constant struggle between the instincts of the id trying to surface and the watchful eye of the superego trying to prevent this from happening, the individual develops the third component of his personality—the ego. The ego is the psychological end result of the compromise between the pressures arising from the instinctual side of our nature and those arising from the social environment which have been forced upon us by authority figures.

Because the id is unable to satisfy its need for a direct outlet due to opposition from the superego, the ego comes into existence to enable the id to achieve a more acceptable outlet. While the id operates through the pleasure principle, the ego's guiding dictum is the reality principle.

The ego essentially sits in judgment of the id and the superego and determines what instincts will be satisfied and how that satisfaction will occur. As a middleman, it is subject to so much pressure that sometimes the ego becomes very anxious. In handling this anxiety, the ego makes use of a number of psychological defenses. We have already encountered one of these defenses in repression. Two other defenses that warrant attention are sublimation and vicarious satisfaction, which have also been previously mentioned. These defense mechanisms enable the id and the superego to live with one another, and, in so doing, they help reduce the anxiety felt by the ego in its role as arbiter between the two.

By means of sublimation the psychic energy in the id that might otherwise be repressed is diverted into some activity that is condoned by the superego. Freud contended that Leonardo da Vinci, for example, sub-

limated his incestuous desires for his mother by painting pictures of Madonnas.

Closely related to sublimation is vicarious satisfaction. Instead of allowing an unacceptable impulse to
be acted out physically, the ego allows that impulse
to be satisfied in a way that does not cause bodily
harm to the victim but still causes him pain. Making
someone the brunt of a joke is one way of venting
hostility on that person without actually striking him.

The Freudian framework involving the conflict between the id and the superego, and the resolution of
this conflict by the ego, has been applied to the writing of graffiti by Allen Dundes, professor of anthro-
pology at the University of California, Berkeley.[7]
Dundes argues that the "psychological motivation for
writing latrinalia is the infantile desire to play with
feces and to artistically smear it around." The basis
for this theory comes from a paper written by Freud's
well-known biographer, Ernest Jones, who is himself
an eminent psychoanalyst.[8]

In this paper, referred to by Dundes, Jones contends that activities such as carving initials or names
on tree trunks are essentially sublimated forms of a
primitive impulse akin to the pleasure infants derive
from playing with their feces, a pleasure that is very
quickly censured by parents intent on cleanliness.
Although Jones did not address himself to the question of latrinalia, Dundes has done this for him in arguing that the motivation for writing on toilet walls stems
from this same primitive smearing impulse described
by Jones. This theory, Dundes asserts, accounts for
the fact that much of the content of lavatory graffiti
refers to defecation and urination. By writing these
"dirty" words upon the walls, the graffiti writers are
symbolically giving vent to their unconscious wish to

play with their own waste matter. As support for this theory, Dundes cites the following traditional verses of latrinalia:

> Those who write on shit house walls
> Roll their shit in little balls
> Those who read these words of wit
> Eat the little balls of shit

Here in these ubiquitous verses, Dundes contends, "is an explicit equation of the act of writing on walls with the manipulation of one's own feces." While this smearing impulse is present in all people, Dundes asserts that the wish to play with one's waste is typically sublimated into more acceptable activities symbolically related to playing with the feces such as finger painting, clay modeling, making mud pies, and so on. Yet another symbolic rechanneling of this impulse takes the form of saying or writing "dirty" words.

There are a number of comments I would like to make concerning this theory. The first involves Dundes's or rather Jones's premise that there is a primitive smearing impulse in each of us because every child plays with his feces. If one follows this line of thinking, then we must also assume that everyone has a drooling impulse because all children drool. Or that we all have a crying impulse because all children cry.

Rather than being specific instincts, are these behaviors not symptomatic of some other underlying factor? Children cry for a number of reasons, one of which is hunger. They drool because they have not learned to control their salivary flow. And they play with their feces not because they have an innate smearing impulse but because they are instinctively curious.

If the concept of instinctual impulses is to retain any validity, then instincts or impulses ought not to be multiplied at will or whim. Thus we are not taking issue with Dundes's general point that latrinalia represents some form of sublimated acting-out process, but rather with what the actual innate pressure for such behavior might be. While Dundes regards the smearing impulse as being responsible for the writing of graffiti, we contend that there is no such thing as a distinct smearing impulse. Instead, smearing as it is observed in children is a manifestation of a more basic instinct—curiosity.

NOTES

1. Sigmund Freud, *A General Introduction to Psychoanalysis* (New York: Washington Square Press, 1963). Although Freud's basic conceptual framework is still the foundation for modern psychoanalytical theory, many of his concepts have been modified by his followers. Known as neo-Freudians, psychoanalysts such as Karen Horney (*Neurotic Personality of Our Times* [New York: Norton, 1937]), Harry Stack Sullivan (*The Interpersonal Theory of Psychiatry* [New York: Norton, 1953]), and Eric Fromm (The Sane Society [New York: Holt, Rinehart and Winston, 1955]), place less emphasis on innate factors and tend to stress instead social and cultural influences on development.

Two contemporaries of Freud's who adopted a more rigid view of the determinants of behavior were the Russian physiologist Ivan Pavlov and the American psychologist John B. Watson. Through his experimental work on learning in animals, Pavlov (*Conditioned Reflexes* [London: Oxford University Press, 1927]) contended that conditioned reflexes formed as a result of experience are the basis for behavioral characteristics. Watson (*Behaviorism* [Chicago: University of Chicago Press, 1959], p. 104) was greatly impressed by Pavlov's research on the development of conditioned reflexes. During the early decades of the twentieth century, Watson conducted various studies of conditioning in human babies at Johns Hopkins University in Baltimore, which convinced him that learning is the only relevant contribution to development: "Give me a dozen healthy infants, well-formed, and my own specified world to bring them up in, and I'll guarantee to take any one at random and train him to become any type of specialist I might select—doctor, lawyer, artist, merchant, chef, and yes, even beggarman and thief, regardless of his talents, penchants, tendencies, abilities, vocations, and race of his ancestors."

Watson's contention that environment is the only important factor in development, however, was never really accepted as an alternative to Freud's theory, since it was too oversimplified. It failed to appreciate the fact that children do differ in their abilities and their responsiveness to the environment. Nevertheless, Watson's radical approach to development did affect subsequent thinking on the influences shaping personality development.

2. James Olds, and P. Milner, "Positive Reinforcement Produced by Electrical Stimulation of Septal and Other Regions of Rat Brain," *Journal of Comparative and Physiological Psychology,* 47 (1954), 419-427.

3. Compare P. M. Milner, *Physiological Psychology* (New York: Holt, Rinehart and Winston, 1970); R. F. Thompson, *Foundations of Physiological Psychology* (New York: Harper & Row, 1967). Disturbances in human sexual behavior have been noted following damage (for instance, tumors, vascular lesions) to the limbic area of the brain. This system, which at one time was called the smell brain (see Chapter 5), includes the lower areas of the frontal lobes, portions of the temporal lobes, the cingulate gyrus, the septal area, the diencephalon, and portions of the upper brain stem. Interestingly, the major change resulting from damage to these areas is not in the ability to engage in physical

sexual activity, but rather the tendency to speak more openly and explicitly concerning such behavior (see E. A. Weinstein, "Sexual Disturbances After Brain Injury," *Medical Aspects of Human Sexuality,* 8 [1974], 10-31).

4. For a discussion of this disease see A. K. Shapiro and E. Shapiro, "Sexuality and Gilles de la Tourette's Syndrome," *Medical Aspects of Human Sexuality*, 9 (1975), 100-125; S. W. Olds, "A Nightmarish Disease," *Today's Health,* 7 (1975), 40-45.

5. Carl Jung, *Collected Works* (Princeton, N.J.: Princeton University Press, 1953).

6. John G. Bourke, *Scatologic Rites of All Nations* (Washington, D.C.: W. H. Loudermilk & Company, 1891).

7. Allen Walker Dundes, "Here I Sit," *Kroeber Anthropological Society,* 34 (1966), pp. 91-105.

8. Ernest Jones, "Anal-Erotic Character Traits," in *Papers on Psychoanalysis* (Boston: Beacon Press, 1961), pp. 413-437.

3 CURIOSITY KILLED THE CAT AND SPAWNED THE GRAFFITO

Regardless of how upset parents may be to discover their children handling, smelling, or tasting their excretions, all children engage in such activities during their infancy. It is not because of any instinctual drive to smear their feces that they do so, however, but rather because of a natural curiosity to discover what this matter is really like.

If one wishes to speak of instincts, then surely curiosity should be so regarded. Curiosity is an inborn characteristic not only of children but of all animals. Rats will learn a maze, for instance, simply for the chance to see, smell, or feel something new.[1] Monkeys will learn to solve intricate puzzles, simply for the opportunity to have a peek at something they have not seen before.[2]

Children are likewise a curious lot. In an experiment conducted at Purdue University, psychologists C. D. Smock and B. G. Holt conducted a simple experiment to study the curiosity drive in five-year-old grammar school children.[3] Each child was placed before a TV screen and shown that whenever he pushed one button, the same picture would always reappear on the screen for a quarter of a second, whereas pushing another button allowed him to see a completely different picture each time. Invariably the children pressed the button that put on the new picture. The results of this experiment are not very surprising, but they do prove the impression that children are very curious beings.

For very young children, with limited experience with the world, their own bodies and the waste products they produce are fascinating playthings. Touching, rubbing, flinging, smearing, smelling, tasting, are all part of discovering the nature of things. It is all part of the curiosity drive that is so basic to life whatever our age. The fact that curiosity is so basic to human life, and is found in nearly all animals, is surely proof that curiosity is indeed an instinct.

Children who grow up in a home where toilet training is begun at a reasonable age and is carried out by parents who do not become overly upset when their children "dirty" themselves have an opportunity to satisfy their curiosity about their waste matter. Once that curiosity is satiated, they lose interest and look around for other objects to explore. When curiosity remains unsatisfied, however, the child or the adult keeps coming back to the object of his curiosity in one way or another. It is as though there is a need to finish what has previously been started.

Psychologists refer to the motivation of many people to remember something until they have finished with it as the Zeigarnik effect, after the man who first described it. Zeigarnik is said to have gotten this idea from watching the waiters in Berlin's sidewalk cafes during the 1920s. In those days waiters did not write their orders down on paper. Instead, they remembered who ordered what and they kept the bill accurately in their heads. But just a short while after the bill had been paid, the same waiters were unable to remember what their customers had previously ordered. It was as if there was a tension associated with the unfinished order, Zeigarnik said, which kept each waiter's mind focused on the bill. Once that tension was discharged, the waiter forgot the whole incident.[4]

In much the same way the curiosity each individual exhibits concerning his waste during his early childhood creates a tension to continue examining this material until his curiosity is satisfied. If satisfaction does not occur, the tension remains. Due to the imposition of parental authority, however, this satisfaction cannot be experienced directly. The superego will simply not tolerate such an indulgence, and the ego will become highly anxious should any such attempt be made. However, the tension cannot be ignored, and thus the ego must find some outlet for it to be discharged.

One of the ways open to the ego, as we have already mentioned, is vicarious gratification. The id can continue to play with its feces indirectly by the use of words. Words, after all, are symbols. They convey ideas. When you write or say a word, you unconsciously visualize the thing that the word stands for. Thus by resorting to this subterfuge of writing "dirty" words upon a wall, an individual is able to play with his feces symbolically, just as he once actually did as a child. The superego may not be deceived by this subterfuge, but it can live with it.

One of the most elementary taboos about which there is likely to be considerable conflict is the speaking or writing of forbidden words. We have previously mentioned that the editors of the Webster's dictionary refused to include the word *fuck* in the compendium because of the hue and cry its inclusion might have caused. The particular conflict over writing "dirty" words usually occurs most often in children, especially those from middle- and upper-class backgrounds. In such families children are taught that certain words cannot be spoken, although parents rarely offer an explanation of why these words are not to be used. Children are simply told that such words are naughty or not polite. Why they are naughty or impolite is never explained.

Observing that these words have special significance for adults and that by using them they can emotionally shock their parents, children learn that these words can be used to manipulate adults. Children do not even have to know the meaning of these words to recognize that their importance lies not in what they refer to but in their shock value. And from the secretive way they are passed from one child to another, there is no mistaking that these words do indeed have emotive shock power.

The child whose behavior is molded and shaped to conform to numerous social conventions can use these words to challenge at least one of these conventions—language. "Dirty" words are the language of protest; each new "dirty" word is a new weapon in the battle between childhood freedom and adult repression.

Usually, the first "dirty" word a child learns is *shit*. This should not be surprising, since the attention he receives from his parents during toilet training is his first indication of the extent to which *shit* is something repulsive to parents. *Shit* is also one of the first weapons that can be used to control parental behavior.

Renatus Hartogs, author of *Four-Letter Word Games*, describes the case of Andy, a six-year-old child who felt that his mother was neglecting him.[5] She was always "going out" or "getting ready." She was so involved in outside activities that she had little time left for Andy. There was one way to get her attention, however, and that was by making "shit" in his pants. This ploy would gain him at least some of her time and attention.

By releasing his waste at an inappropriate time, the child can thus punish his parents for wrongs, real or imagined. By taking note of the emotional response his "dirt" produces, he discovers that "dirt" is power. Later on, when making "dirt" is no longer feasible because of peer pressure, he gives up this particular device and searches about for an alternative means to carry on the war. It is then that he discovers that the verbal symbol for "dirt" can be just as potent as the object it stands for.

The graffiti writer who points out that "Those who write on shit house walls/Roll their shit in little balls" is essentially stating that the act of writing on toilet walls is, for some people, a substitute for playing with their feces. The writer of those verses and the writers to whom he is referring are all in a sense reliving their childhoods. They are satisfying their curiosity about their bodily products by once more playing with their feces. The equation feces equals graffiti is one that has been repeated over and over again not only by the verses just cited but in many other related forms as well:

Some people come here to take a stink
Some people come here to sit and think
But I come here to rub my balls
And read the shit on the walls

Why don't you shit in the toilet
And not on the wall

Somebody take the shit off the walls
and let's start over again

The caretaker
wept as well he might
to see the walls
covered with shit[6]

You who instead of Fodder, Fingers use,
Pray lick 'em clean and don't this wall abuse[7]

But writing *shit* on toilet walls goes beyond simply satisfying one's curiosity. Locked in a toilet stall, an individual is able to challenge once again the authoritarian rules that have been forced upon him. Since language is also something imposed upon him by authoritarians such as his parents, we can recognize these utterances of unacceptable words as basically antiauthoritarian protests. The fact that the walls themselves are owned by someone else makes the obscene graffito doubly antiauthoritarian—through the use of tabooed language and the defacement of the property of another.

NOTES

1. B. T. Leckart, and K. S. Bennett, "Reinforcement Effects of Food and Stimulus Novelty," *Psychological Record,* 18 (1968), 253-260.

2. R. A. Butler, "Incentive Conditions Which Influence Visual Exploration," *Journal of Experimental Psychology,* 48 (1954), 19-23.

3. C. D. Smock, and B. G. Holt, "Children's Reactions to Novelty—An Experimental Study of Curiosity Motivation," *Child Development,* 33 (1962), 631-642.

4. Quoted by C. T. Morgan, and R. A. King, *Introduction to Psychology* (New York: McGraw-Hill, 1966), p. 146.

5. Renatus Hartogs, *Four-Letter Word Games* (New York: Dell Publishing Company, 1967), p. 94.

6. A. W. Read, *Lexical Evidence from Folk Epigraphy in Western North America* (Paris: Privately published, 1935), p. 72.

7. R. Reisner and L. Wechsler, *Encyclopedia of Graffiti* (New York: Macmillan Publishing Company, 1974), p. 381.

4 THE ANAL BRAG

According to Freud's theory of personality development, the predominance of the id, ego, or super-ego in the total personality of the individual depends upon early experiences in childhood, during which each person moves through five separate stages, each of which is associated with a particular source of gratification.[1]

The earliest stage is the oral phase. This is the time that the infant derives all of its pleasure from its mouth through sucking and feeding. By the end of the infant's first year, the next stage begins. This is the anal phase. Since this phase is of direct relevance to the whole phenomenon of graffiti, this period in the infant's development is worth examining at some length.

The anal region is that part of the body through which undigested food materials are eliminated from the body. As these undigested products accumulate in the intestinal tract, they begin to exert pressure on the anal sphincters, a group of muscles that keep this material from leaving the body. As this pressure mounts, a point is eventually reached where the tension becomes so great on these muscles that they can no longer hold back the material building up in the intestine and they open. When this happens, the waste material is forcibly expelled as feces.

The ability to control the anal sphincter muscles usually does not become possible until the child is about two years old. Around this time, parents usually try to teach their children to exercise this control through a process called toilet training.

Toilet training is an important period in a child's life for reasons other than the control he must master over his bowels. It is also a time when he is usually subjected to parental authority and discipline for the first time. It is a time when he experiences his first serious conflict, a conflict that pits his wish to defecate whenever he feels discomfort (id) against an external authority (superego) that demands that he relieve himself only in a designated area. How this external authority is imposed upon the child and how he reacts to that imposition have enormous implications for his later personality.

For example, some parents may be especially patient with their child and they may praise him excessively whenever he confines his waste matter to the toilet. If an "accident" should happen, they do not become overly upset. Other parents may be overly fastidious. They are repulsed by human waste and they place enormous pressure on the child to confine his elimination to the toilet.

These general attitudes may then affect the ways in which the individual later reacts to his waste and the organs that make waste. In the case of the child whose parents praise him excessively for "going to the potty," the anal phase is a time when he enjoys both the erotogenic impulses originating from his rectum and the attention he receives from his parents. The physiological and psychological pleasures may then become so closely associated that each unconsciously acts as a cue for the other.

In other words, each time the individual defecates, the act unconsciously brings to mind the attention and praise he once received from his parents. Conversely, praise and attention unconsciously call to mind the early success at toilet training. Some people who become fixated at the anal stage retain an excessive interest in the act and products of their own defecation for the rest of their lives although they are usually unaware of this narcissism. Nevertheless, the enjoyment, pleasure, satisfaction, and so on, that they derive from this aspect of self-love is readily apparent in those graffiti that call attention to the writer's excretory achievements:

> Some come here to sit and think
> And some come here to wonder
> But I come here to shit and stink
> And fart away like thunder

or to his laments about not being able to fulfill his desires:

> Here I sit all broken hearted
> Paid a nickel only farted

> Here I sit all broken hearted
> Came to shit and only farted

Other traditional graffiti are essentially an effort on the part of the writer merely to call our attention to the "blissful" workings and issue of his rectum:

> Here I sit in silent bliss
> Listening to the falling piss
> Now and then a fart is heard
> In among the thundering turd

> Here I sit in silent bliss
> Listening to the trinkling piss
> Now and then a fart is heard
> Calling to the coming turd

The relief from tension is something that gives everyone a certain amount of pleasure. For the child who is learning to control his bowel movements, the sensation of a large mass of feces passing through his anus and the relief he suddenly feels constitute one of the first real achievements in life. For the first time he has discovered a means of obtaining gratification without having to rely on any other person. It is not surprising, therefore, that a child may not want to have this pleasurable experience regulated by some outside force. Yet this is exactly what happens during toilet training.

The satisfaction that comes from relieving tension in the rectal area has not gone unnoticed in graffiti, although invariably graffiti writers lament that not enough people recognize or appreciate how comforting or satisfying this form of tension release actually is:

> One of the most underestimated pleasures in the world is a good shit

> Americans can't appreciate a good shit, they place too much attention on a good lay

> Good shitting can make me very happy, sometimes more so than fucking

> There is nothing so overrated as a bad fuck and nothing so underrated as a good shit[2]

The reason for this general lack of appreciation is that indiscriminate gratification, such as that which comes from evacuation of bowel and bladder, is not permitted by the superego. Through the long drawn-out process of toilet training, the superego instills the feeling that anything connected with elimination cannot be endowed with any pleasurable sensation. Should such pleasure become associated with the tension-reducing effects of elimination, then the id might attempt to experience that pleasure whenever it might so desire, instead of at an appropriate time and place. This simply cannot be permitted, and to ensure that it never does happen the superego places such anxiety on the ego that the latter is forced to repress any recognition that defecation can be an enjoyable experience. Sometimes, however, the repression is not complete, as indicated in the remarks of the previously cited graffiti writers.

As these graffiti writers point out, most Americans remain unaware (that is, they have repressed their awareness) that making "dirt" can be pleasurable. This is because most American parents tend to be overly fastidious about toilet training. Cleanliness is something that most Americans strive for in their homes and in their children. The young child who tracks dirt into the home typically receives a scolding from his mother. Dirt, he is told, must not be brought into the house. The child who dirties himself with his own waste is also likely to receive a reprimand, the severity of which will depend upon his age and the tolerance and patience of the parents themselves toward such "dirt." This concern over dirt is thus instilled in the child at a very early age and is always present whether one acknowledges or successfully represses the pleasure originally derived from the act of defecation:

> Here I sit broken hearted
> Paid a nickel, only farted
> Yet think of the man who took a chance
> Tried to fart but shit in his pants

First graffiti writer: Here I sit all broken
                            hearted
                            Paid my nickel, only
                            farted

Second graffiti writer: You should squwak,
                         you had your chance
                         I had no nickel and
                         shit in my pants

Here I sit in putrid vapor
Searching for the toilet paper

Here I sit in stinking vapor
Some son of a bitch stole the toilet paper

Upon reading the last two couplets, one wonders whether the reader, coming across them in their usual setting, does not chuckle to himself and then turn anxiously toward the paper dispenser with a misgiving that he may soon share the writers' misfortune. Within these couplets, then, there is a veiled affirmation of the anxiety that accompanies the unpleasant thought of "dirtying" oneself. The following specimens should also be viewed in this context:

No matter how you dance and prance
The last few drops go down your pants

However hard you shake your peg
The last drop will run down your leg

While you are reading this
You are peeing on your shoes

The following are some related graffiti translated

from the Spanish entries in A. Jimenez's book *Picardia Mexicana*:[3]

> No matter how brave you are
> or how much of a man you
> think you are, when you
> get here you get dirty
> or at least you get wet

Note the reference to the unmanliness of "dirtying" one's self. The following dialogue adds some amusement to the situation:

> I hung my good coat
> up in this place and when
> it fell it got all dirty,
> so Mr. Proprietor,
> please put a hanger in here
> and don't mess the place up

(underneath of which was written):

> Even though I'm not a poet
> I am going to answer you.
> One comes here to shit
> and not to hang up your coat

Admittedly these foreign graffiti do not convey any apparent anxiety on the part of their authors, but they do suggest that a concern for avoiding "dirt" was in the minds of these writers when they applied pen or pencil to wall.

Related to this theme of "dirtying" one's self are those ubiquitous graffiti allegedly written by the proprietor, which admonish his customers not to profane the toilet:

Don't throw butts in the urinal
Do we piss in your ash trays?

It's our aim to please
You aim too please

Sometimes the thoughts are not directed to any particular individual but simply express annoyance or
anxiety about "dirtying" one's self:

If your hose is short
And your pump is weak
Stand a lot closer
Or you'll pee on your feet.

Stand closer. The next guy may have holes in
his shoes

Stand up close. The next man may be bare-
footed.

The plea not to urinate on the floor has its counter-
part in the exhortation not to foul the toilet seat:

Men since we all have to use this throne
Kindly keep it clean and neet
Shit down the hole; God damn your soul
And not upon the seat

Here is the place we all must come
To do the work that must be done
So do it quick and do it neat
And for God's sake, not on the seat

Stand on your ass
Not on your feet
Shit down the hole
Not on the seat

This little home is not your own
So try and keep it nice and neat
Bear this in mind and be so kind
That you don't leave a mess here on the seat

Be like brother
Not like Sis
Lift the seat
When you take a piss

Some patrons take a dim view of those who are inconsiderate in this regard:

A man that will stand with his cock
in his hand and piss all over the seat
he ought to be thrashed
his old cock smashed
And his ass kicked out in the street[4]

Despite the fact that many of these graffiti are humorous and seem bereft of any anxiety, the theme that unifies them all is the concern with getting "dirty." Labeling such graffiti as "dirty" is thus not an inappropriate description, since they clearly deal in the language of dirt. Nor is the word *obscene* inappropriate, since etymologically, it comes from the Latin, *ob*, meaning over, and *caenum*, meaning filth. These graffiti, as we have already noted, are essentially symbolic dirt.

NOTES

1. Compare Sigmund Freud, *Three Essays on the Theory of Infant Sexuality* (New York: Avon, 1962).

2. R. Reisner and L. Wechsler, *Encyclopedia of Graffiti* (New York: Macmillan Publishing Company, 1974), p. 214.

3. A. Jimenez, *Picardia Mexicana* (Mexico: B. Costa-Amil, 1958), pp. 102-103.

4. A. W. Read, *Lexical Evidence from Folk Epigraphy in Western North America* (Paris: Privately published, 1935), p. 43.

5 GRAFFITI AS INSPIRATION

While there is no lack of explanation for why people write graffiti, very few social scientists have addressed the problem of what it is about a toilet wall that gets the graffitist to write in the first place. Vicarious gratification, the opportunity to satisfy unfulfilled desires to play symbolically with human waste, accounts for much of what appears on the walls. Anonymity guarantees that the graffitist will not be held accountable for his actions. Psychic conflict and preoccupations affect what the graffitist writes about. But what is the spark that sets the graffitist off?

According to a study conducted by Linda D. Rhyne and Leonard P. Ullman of the department of psychology at the University of Illinois, at Urbana, one out of every fifteen college men writes graffiti in toilets. Rhyne and Ullman asked themselves whether males were inspired to write graffiti by the presence of other graffiti on the wall, or were they just as likely to take pen in hand to a bare toilet wall. In other words, they wanted to find out whether a virgin wall was more or less likely to attract attention as one that had already been deflowered.

To conduct this study the psychologists hired graduate and undergraduate students to remain in the toilet and to enter each stall immediately after it had been vacated. The students were to note whether any inscriptions had been left and to remove any such inscriptions and then wait for the next patron. After counting the number of inscriptions in each instance, the psychologists found that the male graffiti writer is not influenced by the condition of the wall he writes on. He is just as likely to inscribe his thoughts on a virgin as on a deflowered wall. Therefore, toilet wall equals woman is not a factor in graffiti.

Around the turn of the century, a German graffitiologist proposed a rather interesting theory to explain why some people write graffiti in toilets. According to Hugo Luedecke, the air inside a toilet is in some way responsible for the poetry that they scribble on lavoratory walls.[2] Luedecke classified writers of graffiti into two categories: (1) the intellectuals, who write their messages in poetry, and (2) the commoners, who write in prose.

However, Luedecke admitted that commoners are capable of writing verse on occasion, and to account for what to him was a singular accomplishment he proposed that these specially endowed commoners become inspired by their excrement. Just as dogs go about the streets sniffing and exploring the excrement and eventually become excited by the odor of a bitch in heat, so too do these commoners become excited by the smell of human waste. These smells give them so much pleasure and excitement that they feel inspired and in this state they become capable of putting their thoughts into verse.

While Luedecke's theory may seem preposterous to most people, the inspirational theme itself seems to have some appeal to graffiti writers themselves. Consider therefore these lines written on this side of the Atlantic:

Pity the man whose wisdom and wit
Are inspired only
By the sweet smell of shit.

Ridiculous? Nonsense? Poppycock? Or is there something after all to this inspiration idea?

Psychologists, physiologists, zoologists, sexologists, and many other scientists who have made a
study of the influence of odors on behavior have frequently pointed out that the primitive parts of the human brain that are concerned with emotionality are
primarily concerned with smell in more primitive animals. Although this part of the central nervous system
is presently called the limbic system, at one time it
was actually referred to as the smell brain.

This smell brain, which is present in all human
beings, has been inherited from the lower animals
during the course of evolution. In human beings, however, smell is no longer its primary function. Instead,
as a result of its close association with the hypothalamus, it regulates or controls emotional feeling
among other things. During the course of evolution,
the brains of the more highly developed creatures
such as human beings underwent great changes, and
the hypothalamus, which had hitherto been under the
control of the smell brain, now became subject to a
more complex part of the brain, the frontal lobes.

The frontal lobes are responsible for all the complex functions characteristic of human behavior such
as thought, memory, learning, and so on. While the
frontal lobes are capable of overriding any instinctual
responses set into motion by the primitive smell brain,
scientists are still uncertain to what extent this primitive part of our brains still affects emotional dis-
charges from the hypothalamus. In other words, while

human beings are usually able to control their impulses to perform certain acts, they are often not as capable of controlling how they feel about many things, and it is possible that this inability to control our emotions may be a carry-over from our more primitive ancestors on the evolutionary ladder.

The acute sensitivity of animals to odors is well known. For many animals, odors form an olfactory code. These odors, or pheromones as scientists call the actual substances in smells, carry sensory information from one animal to another.[3]

One of the more important messages conveyed by pheromones in the animal world is territoriality. When certain animals wish to stake out a territory as their own, they will urinate, defecate, or simply brush up against a rock, tree, or some other object with their scent glands. The smells they leave on these objects tell all other animals that can "read" the smell to stay away—"this field belongs to me!"

A mouse taken from one cage and placed in another, for example, will immediately be attacked by the residents of the new cage. However, if urine from the new cage is rubbed on the intruder's fur beforehand, the mouse will be treated as a member of the cage. The familiar smell contained in the urine indicates that the bearer of this odor is a friend, a member of the group, and he will not be molested.[4]

While pheromones can elicit or inhibit fighting in animals, their amazing influence over sexual behavior in animals is even more dramatic. Female mice, for instance, become very excited if the urine from a male mouse is put into their cage. Several years ago, psychologists discovered an even more surprising fact about pheromones and female mice. If a male partner was taken away from a female within two days after she had become pregnant and a strange male was brought into her cage, the pregnancy would be spontaneously aborted.[5] Apparently, the odor of the original male partner is necessary for pregnancy to continue at least for the first few days after insemination in mice.

In a more highly developed animal, the monkey, scientists have found that certain substances in the vagina that are secreted by females cause male monkeys instinctively to become very sexually excited.[6] These same substances are also present in the human vagina, and some sexologists such as Alex Comfort, author of the best-seller *Joy of Sex*, speculate that as in monkeys these substances may affect the sexual attractiveness of women to the opposite sex.[7] However, due to the development of the front lobes, the instinctual excitement that these smells arouse in the male are usually overridden by long years of learning to inhibit any overt sexuality. This does not mean, on the other hand, that the desire or emotions associated with sex are not set into motion by these smells.

It is now known that one of the main pheromones that acts as a sexual attractant in odors is musk, the same scent that perfume manufacturers have been loading into their products for years. Is it possible that these distillers of fragrances know more about what "turns on" a man or a woman than the scientists and that only recently have the scientists begun to catch up to the perfume makers? Whatever the answer, we should note before going on that the word *musk* itself comes from ancient Sanskrit, in which it had the meaning "testicle."

According to Comfort, there is in fact considerable evidence that odor plays an important part in human sexuality.[8] For example, he notes that women tend to be much more sensitive in their ability to detect musk about two weeks after menstruation, when they are ovulating, than at any other time of the month. This means that a woman's sense of smell is most acute when she is most susceptible to becoming pregnant. From a biological standpoint this may mean that women are more likely to become excited by the odor of men when they are ovulating. By this ploy, nature increases the probability of survival of the human species.

The ability to detect odors is also influenced by sexual condition in men. Before they reach puberty, boys are barely able to detect the odor of musk. Once they reach sexual maturity, however, boys are clearly able to recognize this previously undetectable odor.

Other sexologists go even further and point out that for some people there is a clear-cut relationship between their noses and sexuality. Marc Hollender, chairman of the department of psychiatry at Vanderbilt University, has noted that in Roman times a man's virility was often judged by the length of his nose.[9] Hollender, a psychiatrist, has found that changes in the condition of the nasal passages actually occur in some women as a result of sexual activity, menstruation, or pregnancy.[10]

Hollender is not the first physician to observe such changes. Even before the turn of the century, physicians were reporting in medical journals that some of their female patients had nosebleeds during menstruation while other patients experienced increased nasal secretions or sneezing during sexual intercourse.[11] These nasal changes were sometimes referred to as the bride's cold.

In 1897 William Fleiss, a close friend of Freud's, claimed that he had discovered "genital spots" in the nose. Addressing the gynecological societies of Berlin and Vienna, Fleiss claimed that he had affected a partial cure for menstrual disorders by applying cocaine, which was then used primarily as a local anesthetic, to the noses of his female patients.[12] At that time, however, his colleagues said that his patients had been cured not by any drug treatment to their noses, but rather as a result of suggestion: It was believed that Fleiss's reassurance, in other words, not his drug, had cleared up the obvious psychosomatic problem of these women.

Despite the ridicule attached to such investigations in recent years, some scientists have continued to study nasal-genital relationships, and their findings show that the nose is indeed a barometer of sex in certain individuals. Norman D. Fabricant,[13] for instance, has shown that after sexual intercourse the temperature inside the nose of adult males goes up from 3.5 to 6.5° F. The change is caused by the dilation of the blood vessels in the nose. This in turn brings more blood into this area and the increased blood supply causes the temperature inside the nose to increase. There is, then, a physiological link between the nose and sexual behavior for some people.

Because of their association with certain settings, persons, or events, odors often call to mind vivid remembrances of past experiences as well. Just as Pavlov's dogs salivated when they heard the sound of a metronome that had been repeatedly associated with food, so too does the smell of certain foods make our mouths water.

Some smells cause us to become alert. They tell the brain that something pleasant or unpleasant is in our vicinity. The relationship between smell and sex in humans is only now being explored in a systematic fashion by scientists, although anthropologists have long referred to the importance of smell in the sexual lives of primitive tribes.

In psychoanalytical theory, as we have already

noted, the individual is assumed to pass through oral, anal, and phallic stages before passing on to adult sexuality. During the anal phase, when they are learning to restrain biological functions, it is not unusual to see young children touching and inspecting their excretions. But not only do these children feel and see, they also smell. According to psychoanalytical theory, if sexual development becomes arrested at the anal stage, the smell of excreta may take on pleasurable sensations and, by association with the anal-erogenous zone, it too may become eroticized.

We have already mentioned that the Romans regarded a long nose as an outward sign of masculinity. This link between the nose and the sex organ may thus have come about as a result of an undue fascination of these people with the smell of excrement. There is, in fact, historical support for such a belief, according to a Spanish author named Torquemada, who wrote at length about the manners of the Romans and Egyptians. "As St. Clement wrote to St. James the Less," Torquemada states, these people

> used to adore stinking and filthy privies and water closets; and, what is viler and yet more abominable, and an occasion for our tears and not to be borne with so much as mentioned by name, they adore the noise and wind of the stomach when it expires from itself and cold or flatulence and other things of the same kind, which according to the same saint, it would be a shame to name or describe.[14]

It is also worth noting in this context that the Romans actually worshiped gods who ruled eliminative functions.[15]

The symbolic relationship between the nose and sex has been commented on by several psychoanalysts.[16] In one of the more notable cases in the medical literature, Freud told us about a patient of his whom he referred to as the "Wolf Man." The man felt that his nose was considerably disfigured. As analysis continued to peel away the layers of repression, it became clear that the man had symbolically equated his nose with his penis and that it was his apprehension about his genital that lay at the root of his fears.[17]

Hollender cites the case of a male homosexual who requested a "nose job" from a plastic surgeon. When asked to draw a picture of the kind of nose he wanted, the man proceeded to outline the profile of a woman's nose.[18] Another case cited by Hollender is that of a nineteen year old who was suffering a great deal of anxiety because he masturbated. To relieve himself of these feelings he asked that the bone be removed from his nose because he felt that it was too prominent. By submitting to such an operation, he hoped that he would then have a softer nose (penis).[19]

Having digressed somewhat in examining the importance of smells with respect to aggressiveness and especially sex, let us return to those graffiti that deal with the theme of smells. We have already noted that most graffiti writers describe the odor of excrement as being stinking or putrid. However, there are those who find the smell of excrement sweet, as the writer of the previously mentioned lament points out, pitying the man whose wisdom and wit "are inspired only by the sweet smell of shit."

The descriptive adjective *sweet* may seem totally out of place in the context of waste matter, but consider this excerpt from the notes of a physician of the seventeenth century who described a patient he had examined:

A boy of four years old had fouled in bed; but being much afraid of a whipping, he ate his own dung, yet he could not blot the sign out of the sheets; wherefore, being asked by threatenings, he at length tells the chance. But being asked of its savor, he said it was of a stinking and somewhat sweet one.

Another physician relates that "a noble little virgin, being very desirous of her salvation, eats her own dung, and was weak and sick. She was asked of what savor it was, and she answered it was of a stinking and a waterishly sweet one."[20] Apparently, then, the adjective *sweet* is not completely out of place when linked to human waste, at least for some people.

The fact that some people actually enjoy the odors associated with elimination is also apparent in this graffito:

People who like the smell of their own farts
are habitual masturbators.

While the author of these words indicates that he condemns such people, he is at least aware that they do exist. Other graffiti writers indicate that they are enamored by the noises and odors they create:

Fart of my fart
I love that melody
It's a part of me

Perhaps when all is said and done, Luedecke's theory that some people are inspired by the smells of their waste to write graffiti may not be so far-fetched after all.[21]

NOTES

1. Linda D. Rhyne and Leonard P. Ullmann, "Graffiti: A Nonreactive Measure," *Psychological Record,* 22 (1972), 157-168.

2. Hugo Luedecke, "Grundlagen der Skatologie," *Anthropophyteia* 7 (1907), 316-328.

3. Compare I. Eibl-Eibesfeldt, *Ethology* (New York: Holt, Rinehart and Winston, 1975).

4. R. A. Mugford and N. W. Nowell, "The Preputial Glands as a Source of Aggression Promoting Odors in Mice," *Physiology and Behavior,* 6 (1971), 247-249.

5. H. M. Bruce, "A Block to Pregnancy in the Mouse Caused by Proximity of Strange Males," *Journal of Reproduction and Fertility,* 1 (1960), 96-903.

6. G. Epple, "Primate Pheromones," in M. C. Birch (ed.), *Pheromones* (London: North Holland Co., 1974), pp. 367-385.

7. Alex Comfort, "The Likelihood of Human Pheromones," in Birch (ibid., pp. 386-396). See also R. A. Schneider, "The Sense of Smell and Human Sexuality," *Medical Aspects of Human Sexuality,* 5 (1971), 157-168.

8. Comfort (ibid).

9. Marc H. Hollender, "The Nose and Sex," *Medical Aspects of Human Sexuality,* 6 (1972), 84.

10. Ibid., 93.

11. J. N. Mackenzie, "The Physiological and Pathological Relations Between the Nose and the Sexual Apparatus of Man," *Johns Hopkins Hospital Bulletin,* 9 (1898), 10-15.

12. Hollender, "The Nose and Sex," p. 99. Freud also speculated on the relationship between the nose and sex on several occasions. On the basis of a patient's symptoms that he treated in 1892, Freud wrote to his colleague William Fleiss in 1897 outlining some of his thoughts on the subject (Letter 55 in *The Origins of Psychoanalysis,* [London: Imago, 1954]). In 1909 he returned to the issue once again: "I should like to raise the general question whether the

atrophy of the sense of smell (which was the inevitable result of man's assumption of an erect posture) and the consequent organic repression of his pleasure in smell may not have had a considerable share in the origin of his susceptibility to nervous disease" (quoted by A. Peto, "The Olfactory Forerunner of the Superego: Its Role in Normalcy, Neurosis, and Fetishism," *International Journal of Psychoanalysis,* 54 (1973), 323-330.

13. N. D. Fabricant, "Effects of Coitus on Nasal Temperature," *Fertility and Sterility,* 11 (1960), 195-200.

14. Quoted in John G. Bourke, *Scatologic Rites of All Nations* (Washington, D.C.: W. H. Loudermilk & Company, 1891), p. 127.

15. Ibid.

16. See, for example, E. Jones, "The Theory of Symbolism," in *Papers on Psychoanalysis* (Baltimore: Williamson and Wilkins, 1948).

17. Quoted in Hollender, "The Nose and Sex," p. 92.

18. Ibid.

19. Ibid.

20. Quoted by Bourke, *Scatologic Rites,* p. 29.

21. The reference to unpleasant smells to denote something amiss has not received very serious study although language contains numerous such examples: "I smell a rat," for instance, indicates trickery and deceit; something "smells to high heaven" when it is clearly underhanded; something "stinks" when it violates a social or moral code; and "something is rotten in the state of Denmark," is Marcellus's acknowledgment of "foul" play in Shakespeare's *Hamlet.*

6 THE LANGUAGE OF GRAFFITI

Just as swearing has some cathartic or purging effect on our pent-up emotions, so does writing a graffito have a similar relief-giving effect for some people. In the words of anthropologist Ashley Montagu, "swearing may be regarded as an emotional orgasm."[1]

If indeed the circumstances that give rise to graffiti are emotional in origin, then it should not be too surprising that emotion-laden words are nearly always used to express these inner feelings. And the most emotionally charged words in our language are those that refer to sex and excretion. These words, like laxatives, have the power to purge.

But why is it that short, monosyllabic words such as *fuck*, *shit*, *fart*, and *cunt* have greater emotional impact than their longer, polysyllabic counterparts—*fornicate*, *defecate*, *flatus*, and *vagina*? The reason is that these four-letter words have broken away from their original meaning and have come to represent antisocial actions or ideas that are essentially nonsexual.

Behavior that involves genital contact but does not result in reproduction has traditionally been socially if not legally proscribed. Among these "unnatural" acts are masturbation, homosexuality, oral-genital intercourse, and sodomy. Except for "self-abuse," all these acts are classified as crimes in the United States, although it is rarely the case that the person or property of another is threatened or damaged.

The basis for their status as crimes is the moral attitude that they are crimes against nature, not crimes against human beings. These crimes against nature carry penalties far more severe than those pronounced on people who act against mankind as a whole by polluting the air and water. This is one of the ironies inherent in our sense of morality.

Apart from the legal penalties, these so-called unnatural sexual acts have been encapsulated in everyday language with a strong visceral connotation. Their respectability, writes Edward Sagarin, is inversely related to some undesirable nonbiological function, although these words all have a biological basis. Besides being "unnatural," these words are "dirty," "perverted," "degenerate," and "immoral." They carry such an emotional charge because they are symbols of objects or behavior that is traditionally restricted to certain times, people, and places.

No word has any significance except by virtue of its symbolic nature. Saying or writing four-letter words conjures up the objects or behavior that they stand for and brings them into consciousness. It forces the person who hears or reads them to imagine that part of the body or that biological act to which they refer and, at the same time, tells him that the speaker or writer is likewise visualizing them. It is as if the speaker or writer is exhibiting himself. This is the reason such language is not permitted in mixed company. Furthermore, this reasoning extends to any behavior that uses sex or elimination or the organs involved in these functions for anything other than what is deemed natural. The use of such images through language in polite company is nothing short of taboo.

Webster's defines the noun *taboo* as something "set apart or (made) sacred by religious custom" or something "forbidden by tradition or social usage or other authority; strongly disapproved as conflicting with conventions, or settled beliefs. . . ." A taboo may be "a sacred interdiction laid upon the use of certain things or words or the performance of certain actions. . . ."

William Graham Sumner, the esteemed student of folkways, defined taboos simply as "things which must not be done."[2] Each society has its taboos, the origins of which are lost in its hoary past, but which it continues to pass on to succeeding generations as traditions and habits. Even if a person's taboos relate only to himself, writes H. Webster, "their observance imposes a restraint on human passions and requires the mastery of self-regarding impulses which otherwise would be irresistible."

This notion of restraint of human passions occurs throughout the literature dealing with the topic of taboo. Freud regarded taboos as prohibitions that were forceably imposed on people for the purpose of keeping in check powerful impulses, the expression of which would disrupt society, but which nonetheless he regarded as constantly seeking release from the part of the unconscious where they were normally trapped.[3] Sumner contends that the passionate nature of the sex appetite so lends itself to excess and vice that it forces society to connect it with taboos.[4]

In the case of language, certain words take on the aura of taboo because they refer to objects or acts that are considered too private to be shared. In Western society the most private of acts are sex and elimination—both of which were once imbued with great religious and mysterious qualities. It is for this reason that four-letter words are so emotionally volatile. They refer directly to something lodged in the mind, something from the archaic past, something invested with mysterious power, something scatological, something venal, yet something sacred. It is taboo to refer to such acts and objects lightly. They must be dignified with euphemism, circumlocutions, technical terms. Why then do we use these potent words, these profane, explosive, emotionally charged symbols?

For some people it is essentially for the excitement of doing the forbidden. There is a perverse pleasure that goes along with breaking a taboo. Forbidden fruit, the maxim says, tastes juiciest. By delving into the dark side of society's psyche, the swearer or graffitist can titillate himself with the thought that he has broken a taboo.

At Central Washington State College in Ellenberg, Washington, two psychologists, Thomas B. Collins and Paul Batzle, were curious to see the effect of explictly prohibiting graffiti on the walls. Accordingly, they posted signs: DO NOT WRITE ON WALLS, on the toilet stalls at the college library and counted the number of graffiti written before and after the signs were put in place. As one might expect if violating a wall is part and parcel of the graffitist's intention, there were twice as many inscriptions appearing after the signs went up as before.[5]

But to what extent do we have to fear the language of taboo? Is censorship of language an archaic remnant of the past? In general, four-letter words are the most volatile and emotion-laden words in the English language, and using them, as Montagu observes, is

merely one form out of a large number of possible learned varieties of hostile or ag-

gressive behavior.... By affording the means
of working off the surplus energy of the emotion induced by frustration, the tension between the emotion and the object of it is
decreased and the final dissolution of the
tension is expressed in a feeling of relief,
which in its place is a sign of the return to a
state of equilibrium.

If swearing does act as a safety valve for pent-up
emotions, then should it not be condoned instead of
proscribed? Is it not better to protect society from the
direct expression of hostility by allowing the language
of taboo a recognized place in society? Whether
spoken or written in graffiti, the language of taboo has
social importance in many ways, in addition to that of
"letting off steam." By investing certain words with
sweeping emotional overtones, we leave the bulk of
language free of apprehension. Taboo words draw all
the flack and excitement and leave other words to do
their job of symbolization and communication without
any fear of embarrassment or censure.[6] Because taboo words are so important in language, they must
be accorded their due respect.

The more frequently the language of taboo is
broken, however, the less titillating the experience.
Taboo words then become part of the normal vocabulary of speech, or they simply disappear through lack
of interest. The safety valve is no longer operative.
The taboo words cease to be scapegoats. Without
something to divert pent-up hostility inoffensively, society places itself in danger of chaos—hence the need
to maintain the taboo.

Graffiti are saturated with taboo words, and one
might expect that those who use them probably derive
a great emotional release from merely writing them.

But in addition to this they allow the graffitist to deface a wall and hence add to his aggressive discharge. The combination of antisocial thought, antisocial language to express it, and antisocial disfigurement of someone else's property enables the graffitist to discharge in one "emotional orgasm" many of the deep-seated emotions he may be harboring and thus helps him to regain his composure.

NOTES

1. Ashley Montagu, *Anatomy of Swearing* (New York: Collier Books, 1967), p. 85.

2. William Graham Sumner, *Folkways* (New York: Dover Press, 1959), p. 43.

3. Compare H. Webster, *Taboo* (Stanford, Calif.: Stanford University Press, 1942), p. 11.

4. Sumner, *Folkways,* p. 298.

5. T. Collins and P. Batzle, "Method of Increasing Graffito Responses," *Perceptual and Motor Skills*, 31 (1970), 733-734.

6. As stated by P. D. McGlynn ("Graffiti and Slogans: Flushing the Id," *Journal of Popular Culture,* 6 [1972], 351-356), graffiti are "rhetorically removed from the obligations of debate. . . . The rhetoric is final and unimpeachable, in a word secure—as secure as the latch on a lavatory wall."

7 IN YOUR HAND RESTS THE FUTURE OF AMERICA

The third stage of psychosexual development begins around age three when the child first begins to associate pleasure with the manipulation of his genitals. Freud referred to this period as the phallic phase and considered it to be the third and last of the pregenital periods consisting of it and the oral and anal phases.

Following the phallic phase comes the latency period, which begins around school age and ends around puberty. The final stage of psychosexual development is called the genital stage. This is the period of growth when sexual relations characteristic of mature adulthood are learned. This chapter will examine in depth the phallic stage, especially as it pertains to graffiti.

In the same way that the child is taught by his parents not to play with his feces, he is also taught not to play with himself. Moreover, the same conditioning factors that result in anxiety becoming attached to the thought of making "dirt" likewise result in anxiety becoming attached to masturbation, which is also called dirty. Other terms that signify society's disapproval of masturbation are *self-abuse* and the *soli-*

tary sin. D. H. Lawrence, who was so instrumental in forcing twentieth-century society to redefine the meaning of obscenity and pornography, was himself horrified and disgusted by this form of sexual behavior. "Instead of being a comparatively pure and harmless vice," he claimed that "masturbation is certainly the most dangerous sexual vice that society can be afflicted with in the long run."

In Western society children are taught at a very early age that masturbation is wrong and will be punished, possibly with castration, if it continues. This injunction against masturbation is part of the centuries' old Judeo-Christian heritage that has its roots in the story of the biblical figure Onan, who was punished with death for spilling his seed upon the ground. *Onanism*, in fact, was a term once used rather widely as a synonym for masturbation. Actually, however, the Bible condemned Onan not for masturbating but for practicing coitus interruptus (withdrawal of the penis just prior to ejaculation), which resulted in his spilling his seed.

Around the middle of the eighteenth century, a French physician named Tissot mistakenly labeled Onan's sin as masturbation in a widely read book entitled *Onana, A Treatise on the Diseases Produced by Onanism* and went on to claim that the habit led, among other things, to a "general wasting away of the body . . . a loss of imagination and memory . . . imbecility . . . [and] a feeling of being an inert weight on earth."

One would think that such nonsense would have been summarily dismissed by the medical profession, but instead not only were Tissot's pronouncements endorsed by succeeding generations of physicians but they were even exaggerated further by those who preferred spreading anxiety to looking into the ques-

tion impassionately and objectively. Certain physicians declared, for example, that masturbation is
widely recognized as a common cause of insanity and
that fatuity, caused by debility of the brain, is in turn
caused by the pernicious habit of masturbation.

The most preposterous statements concerning the
evils of the solitary sin, however, were those issued
by a minister, Sylvanus Stall. Writing in his book, *What
a Young Boy Ought to Know*—which first appeared
in 1897 and subsequently went through several re-
printings, so popular was it—Stall warned of the possibility of genetic damage to the children of men who
indulged themselves in the heinous act:

> The consequences which result from mas-
> turbation do not stop with the boy who prac-
> tices it, nor with his parents, brothers and
> sisters, friends and relatives, but where such
> a boy lives to become a man, if he marries,
> and should become a father, his children
> after him must suffer to some measurable
> degree the results of his sin. . . . As in grain
> so in human life, if the quality of the grain
> which is sown in the field is poor, the grain
> that grows from it will be inferior. When a
> boy injures his reproductive powers, so that
> when a man his sexual secretion shall be of
> an inferior quality, his offspring will show it
> in their physical, mental, and moral natures.
> So you see that even a young boy may pre-
> pare the way to visit upon his children that
> are to be, the results of vices and sins com-
> mitted long years before they were born.
> This is surely a very impressive thought.[1]

In case Stall's remarks would go unnoticed by those

who could not read, he recorded his warning for those who were illiterate but could still afford a phonograph.

Despite the so-called sexual revolution, such ignorance has not been totally erased in the latter half of the twentieth century. In their recent landmark study of human sexual behavior, Masters and Johnson reported that every male they interviewed exhibited a marked concern for the possible deleterious mental affects of excessive masturbation.[2] Not much has changed then, in the past few centuries, since the public is still being taught that masturbation can produce serious physical and mental harm to those who indulge in such a practice.

Among the calamities still being attributed to masturbation, Alfred Kinsey said, are "every conceivable ill from pimples to insanity, including stooped shoulders, loss of weight, fatigue, insomnia, general weakness, neurasthenia, loss of manly vigor, weak eyes, digestive upsets, stomach ulcers, impotence, feeblemindedness, [and] genital cancer."[3]

The insane were often accused of having come to their sorry condition as a result of "self-abuse" and in some asylums those whose insanity was attributed to this alleged vice were kept in separate areas away from other patients for fear that they might contaminate them with their misguided venality. Thousands of inmates were actually kept in strait-jackets in the belief that this would hasten their recovery, since they would not long be able to masturbate. Graffiti that preserve these fears can still be found scribbled on lavatory walls, although they are far less common than was once the case. Some representative examples of this genre are the following:

> I don't care if I go crazy
> As long as I can beat my daisy

Four time more is thirty-two
Three more pulls and I'll be through

She made herself
And called it insanity
I made myself
And call it fun

Jerk off and get more pimples[4]

Interestingly, the term *jerk* is often used in the sense of fool or idiot in common speech, in keeping with the belief that insanity in some cases has its roots in masturbation. Similarly, the expression *pulling my leg* is used to mean that someone is trying to make a fool of someone else. *Pulling* is likewise often used as a synonym for masturbation in graffiti:

Be a man, not a fool
Pull the chain, not your tool

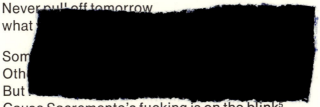

Never pull off tomorrow
what

Som
Oth
But
Cause Sacremento's fucking is on the blink[5]

Two limericks having masturbation as their theme found their way into graffiti at the University of North Carolina at Chapel Hill:

There was a young man from Dulene
Who invented the whip-off machine
On the 99th stroke
The doggone thing broke
And pounded his pecker to cream

There was a young man from Milano
Who loved to play the piano
His fingers did slip
And unzipped his zip
And out popped a hairy banana

Two other examples of graffiti that deal with the masturbation theme without specifying any untoward effects:

This is a teepee
For you to peepee
Not a wigwam
To beat your tomtom

One orgasm in the hand
Is worth two in the bush

A graffito that does express danger from masturbation places it in a racial context:

Here the dual themes of masturbation and interracial union are entwined in such a way that "giving birth to a coloured child" is presented as the punishment for masturbation.

In 1948 Kinsey claimed that over 92 percent of all American adult men have a history of masturbation.[7] More recent surveys have tended to support this relatively high incidence of the practice, indicating that nearly all men masturbate at one time or another. It is clear, then, that despite the warnings and threats with which they have been bombarded, men still continue to masturbate. Few other activities, notes Comfort, have been more frequently discussed, condemned, or practiced than masturbation.[8]

This does not mean, however, that these warnings and threats have not been without effect. "If the child is seriously disturbed over his behavior," Kinsey comments, "the disturbance may color his personality through life." This disturbance usually takes the form of anxiety that can be instilled in various ways, as in cases "where adults discovered the activity, reprimanded or punished the youngster, made a public exhibition of the offense, or upset the child's peace of mind in some other way."[9]

"Even parents who try to avoid reprimands may cause some disturbance in the child," Kinsey pointed out,

> because they, the parents themselves are inhibited, or because they are not accustomed to observing sexual behavior of any sort. It takes no more than a show of surprise on the part of the parent, a supercilious smile, or even a studied avoidance of the issue to make it apparent to the child that the parent is emotionally upset and that sexual activity is in a different category from other everyday affairs.[10]

If masturbation is no longer considered to be a danger to physical or mental health per se, why then is it still so contentiously stigmatized by so many people? The reason, according to Freud, is that masturbation initially begins during the child's phallic stage at a time in his life when he is very attached to his mother. Because of this attachment, a male child feels very possessive of his mother and very jealous of his father, his primary rival for his mother's affections. This desire for his mother and antagonism toward his father Freud called the Oedipus complex.

During the course of his psychiatric practice, Freud had observed that nearly all of his neurotic patients harbored an unconscious incestuous fantasy toward the parent of the opposite sex and a murderous jealousy for the parent of the same sex. Because of the similarity between this mental state and the Greek figure of Oedipus, who without realizing it killed his father and married his mother, Freud named this fantasy after the tragic Greek character. The more he explored the unconsicous mental lives not only of his patients but of normal people as well, however, Freud began to find that this Oedipus complex was present in everyone, not only in those in need of psychiatric help. (In the case of the female, Freud referred to her lustful desire for her father and antagonism for her mother as the Electra complex.)

Should a male child continue to feel sexually attracted to his mother, he will begin to become anxious lest his father, who is much more powerful than he, will take revenge on his son. The form of revenge feared most is castration, the removal of the male sex organ, the symbol of manhood. The possibility that this may in fact take place becomes all the more likely should the child catch a glimpse of the female sexual anatomy, which lacks the male organ. The female, he deduces, has been castrated, and if he does not repress his incestuous desire for his mother, he too will be castrated. In general, this desire for his mother is repressed and the child eventually identifies with his father. If, however, repression does not occur and the child continues to desire his mother, he may have difficulty with heterosexual relationships in later years.

During the phallic stage, the child of course is in no position to compete sexually with any adult. Masturbation, however, substitutes for the direct expression of any sexual impulses the child might feel toward the parent of the opposite sex. During the latency phase of development, masturbation is usually not engaged in or if it is not totally abandoned, it is considerably diminished and does not reappear until puberty and the final genital stage of development.

While the original Oedipal fantasy is repressed by this time, it continues to exert an unconscious influence on mental life so that any time masturbation reoccurs, the Oedipal fantasy is unconsciously recalled and this in turn unconsciously brings up the anxiety concerning castration. It is because of this constant reawakening of the castration anxiety that masturbation continues to be frowned upon. In an attempt to keep this fantasy and anxiety from surfacing into consciousness the superego demands that masturbation be renounced. However, for many individuals this is not easily accomplished.

Since the behavior we have been discussing is so widespread and since it is also generally looked down upon as being "unmanly" or "dirty," it is not surprising that many adults experience recurring conflict and anxiety concerning their own masturbation. Sometimes the guilt associated with masturbation is so great that the individual resorts to other related acts such as excessive scratching, nail biting, nose picking, and other sublimated forms of masturbation.

For those who are unable to stop masturbating for any of a number of different psychological reasons and for whom there may also be a feeling of guilt or shame attached to the knowledge that they are doing something they know is socially frowned upon, there may be a need to express their anxiety. It is possibly for this reason that the theme of masturbation has occurred so frequently in graffiti.

The terms *jerk off* and *pull off*, which we previously encountered in connection with graffiti dealing with masturbation, originate according to Sagarin with an unconscious fear of castration. "The phrases," writes Sagarin, "suggest that something is attached, and by a pulling or jerking motion, the attached piece might become detached."[11]

The fear of castration is a powerful but subconscious motivating factor in the lives of many men according to psychoanalytical theory. Graffiti that deal with this fear allow it to be expressed symbolically and, at the same time, protect the writer from becoming consciously aware of his innermost apprehension. Graffiti thus represent an escape mechanism for some individuals.

The fear of castration also figures in those pervasive graffiti that deal with what G. Legman calls phallic-brag.[12] Usually, these inscriptions deal with the theme of erectile potency:

> My cock is 10 inch. long, come and get it

> I have a eleven inch prick and it is hard all the time[13]

> I am 15 years old. I have a big cock 15 inches long and hair on my belly. I got a hard on now[14]

Occasionally, one may find the beginnings of a survey:

> Check one best answer. My penis is:
> A. Too long
> B. Too short

    C. Missing
    D. Atrophic
    E. None of the above

or a lament:

> Allow me to state in this mournful dirge
> That life has played a terrible trick
> On the man possessed by a giant's urge
> Who is also cursed with pygmy's prick

A graffito exchange that is becoming almost traditional is one that begins by listing the dimensions of the penis:

> I'm 10″ long and 4″ wide

under which someone else invariably writes:

> Fine, but how big is your prick?

In a later chapter we shall see that this transposition of the first writer's meaning amounts to what is really an act of symbolic castration on the part of the second writer, since he doubtless knows to what the first is referring, but he still manages to make the first writer appear to be a fool. By twisting the first writer's meaning, the second writer manages to emasculate him, which is just the opposite of the first writer's intention in describing his oversized organ. In this exchange both writers are essentially expressing their preoccupations on the subject of penile length, and hence the second writer is just as aware of the relationship between manliness and length of the penis as is the first.

Since penile length is particularly a matter of concern to the American male, perhaps a few words are in order on this subject. Sexologists have repeatedly emphasized that penile size has almost no bearing on a man's ability to satisfy a woman sexually. The only exceptions are when the penis is so large that it causes the woman pain by putting pressure on the cervix, or when it is so small that penetration and pelvic contact cannot be achieved.

The width of the penis, on the other hand, may affect the female's enjoyment of intercourse because the wider it is, the more contact it will make with the tissues inside the vagina. This contact causes the clitoris to be pulled and thus stimulates the female organ, thereby causing the female to experience pleasure.

Regardless of what or how often they have been told that there is little or no correlation between penile length and the female's sexual pleasure, men have traditionally regarded a long penis as a *sine qua non* for producing sexual enjoyment in women. It is not uncommon, in fact, to hear of some men who have tried to stretch their penises by tying strings attached to lead weights to their organs.

In 1970 *Forum* magazine published the results of a survey in which male readers sent in measurements of their penises. The longest recorded was 9.5 inches in erection. This corresponds quite closely with reports published by Wardell B. Pomeroy, an associate of the eminent sexologist Kinsey. The longest penis Pomeroy ever observed was 10 inches. However, David Reuben, author of the best-seller *Everything You Always Wanted to Know About Sex*, claims that the largest penis he ever observed was 14 inches. In contrast to these noteworthy specimens, the smallest penis ever recorded (by Kinsey) was 1 inch in length. The *Forum* survey found the smallest penile size among its respondents to be 4.75 inches.

It is very unusual to find any scientific studies that compare the sizes of penises in different societies or cultures. However, author G. L. Simons, compiler of the remarkable *Simons' Book of World Sexual Records*, refers to one such enterprise in which the average Englishman was accorded the dubious distinction of possessing the longest male organ; second were the males of West Germany. Contrary to popular opinion, the black male's penis (7.5 inches) was found to be slightly smaller in erection than the average white male's organ (7.75 inches).[15] However, in his *Sexual Myths and Fallacies* James Leslie McCary refers to scientific investigations involving careful measurement of the male sex organ that showed that "the flaccid penis of the average black male is slightly longer than that of the white man."[16]

McCary notes further that there is no evidence that blacks are more promiscuous than whites. The fact is, McCary states, that promiscuity occurs most frequently among

> poorly educated Americans of low socioeconomic status . . . and since a greater number of black citizens—sadly, a majority, fall into the first group than whites do, many people erroneously conclude that racial, rather than environmental or class, factors account for the differences in sexual activity.[17]

McCary likewise observes that the middle class believes that people from the lower socioeconomic classes are more primitive and aggressive. Since both these traits are popularly associated with sex in the minds of many Americans, this notion exaggerates the idea that blacks are sexually more prolific than whites. And since sexuality is so closely tied to penile size, there is a popular misconception that the black male's sex organ is a battering ram of masculine potency.

A graffito that was once traditional in America that

was a disguised allusion to the male concern with penile potency, but which has almost disappeared, is the picture of the wide-eyed Kilroy with his long banana nose protruding over the fence top. The banana nose is symbolic of the male penis, and the wide eyes are Kilroy's testicles. The announcement that "Kilroy was here" means that Kilroy, or rather the drawer of the face, is still intact. He still has his genitals.

The fact that penile size is a rather major psychological concern for many males is also indicated by the frequency with which psychiatrists are asked about such matters by their patients. The reason for this concern is, as we have repeatedly noted, that the possession of a long penis is the mark of a "real" man. The man with the longest penis is considered to be not only the most masculine but is also deemed to stand out in all areas in which men compete with one another.

Graffiti that portray the penis directly or indirectly, as in the Kilroy example, or that describe the length or erectile potency of the male organ are basically attempts on the part of the artist or writer to reassure himself that he is still a man. The following examples, which revolve around the idea of progenitive prowess, are really reassurances that the male appendage is still intact:

In your hand rests the future of America

with such variants as:

In what you are holding now, lies the future of the world

England's future rests in your hands[18]

The man who holds an erection in his hands in this toilet makes more humans than all the kings of France[19]

At this point, let us return to a discussion of the Oedipus complex and castration anxiety. One of the most laconic of graffiti that relate to these two topics is the expletive *mother fucker.*

The notion of having incestuous desires concerning one's own mother would be intolerable should that thought ever come into consciousness, not only because of the rigid taboos against incest, but also because of the attendant fear that castration will accompany any such relationship. The graffiti writer who places these words on any available wall as often as he can may deceive himself into thinking that he is hurtling defiance at his readers; but the real significance of this repetitive expletive is that it constitutes a disguised yet powerful fear lurking in his subconscious.

Renatus Hartogs, in his *Four-Letter Word Games*, has suggested that this expression contains much greater potency for the black person than the Caucasian,[20] an impression recently borne out by Lee Sechrest, a psychologist at Northwestern University, in Illinois. In a study to be examined in much greater depth in the next chapter, Sechrest found many more instances of the graffito *mother fucker* in the toilets at trade schools than in those in four-year or professional schools.[21] Since the trade schools tend to have a higher enrollment of black students, whereas the opposite is true of the four-year and professional schools, Sechrest's study suggests that the black student does indeed experience more mental conflict over the resolution of his Oedipal fantasies.

The reason for this greater conflict, Hartogs contends,[22] is the environment many blacks grow up in. Because of its poverty the minority family is often forced to live in crowded conditions in which a mother and son may often share the same bed even long into the school years. Growing up under such conditions, a boy may have great difficulty in resolving his Oedipal fantasy to possess his mother sexually, especially since he remains so close to his mother psychologically as well as physically.

Hartogs also points out that in a slum setting, the adult male rarely lives up to his role as a father except insofar as he impregnates his spouse. Usually, he is rarely in the home. Because of the father's absence the school-age boy usually has to take upon himself as much of the father's role as he can shoulder for his age. As acting head of the household, however, he does not enjoy the prerogative of the dominant male toward the adult female. And should his mother herself be polyandrous, his Oedipal desires may have to come to grips with a number of "fathers," all of whom could be potential castrators.

While the term *mother fucker* is still primarily written in the slum area setting, Hartogs contends that it is beginning to gain more currency among the middle class because of the weakening of marriage ties. Extramarital relations are no longer the anathema they once were, and divorce has become commonplace in American society.

Typically, when a couple is divorced, the mother retains custody of the child(ren). When this happens, the middle-class boy is often placed in the same circumstances as the slum-raised child whose father has abandoned the family—he is supposed to assume the dominant male role and at the same time he has to contend with adult male rivals for his mother's affections.

The individual whose graffiti consist to a great extent of writing *mother fucker* may thus be possibly plagued by the fear that he indeed wishes to be one. By writing this on the wall, the graffitist is not consciously admitting his fear, but rather is trying to reassure himself that he does not entertain such desires. The written words are an announcement that he is free from such a revolting idea—it is the reader whom he accuses of this despicable wish. Yet the very pervasiveness of this expletive indicates that the writer and those who share his background and experience are very much preoccupied with the fear that they may indeed harbor such incestuous desires.

NOTES

1. Quoted in Alex Comfort, *Anxiety Makers* (Bristol: Thomas Nelson & Sons, Ltd., 1967), p. 93.

2. W. H. Masters and V. E. Johnson, *Human Sexual Response* (Boston: Little, Brown & Company, 1966).

3. Alfred C. Kinsey, *Sex in the Human Male* (Philadelphia: W. B. Saunders Company, 1948), p. 513.

4. A. W. Read, *Lexical Evidence from Folk Epigraphy in Western North America* (Paris: Privately published, 1935), p. 63.

5. Ibid., p. 49.

6. Ibid., p. 54.

7. Kinsey, *Sex in the Human Male,* p. 499.

8. Comfort, *Anxiety Makers*, pp. 69-113.

9. Kinsey, *Sex in the Human Male*, p. 503.

10. Ibid., pp. 503, 507.

11. E. Sagarin, *Anatomy of Dirty Words* (New York: Paperback Library, 1969), p. 75.

12. G. Legman, *Rationale* (London: Panther Books, 1969), p. 302.

13. Read, *Lexical Evidence,* p. 49.

14. Ibid., p. 57.

15. G. L. Simons, *Simons' Book of World Sexual Records* (New York: Pyramid Books, 1975), p. 55.

16. James Leslie McCary, *Sexual Myths and Fallacies* (New York: Van Nostrand & Company, 1971), p. 43.

17. Ibid., p. 42.

18. R. Freeman, *Graffiti* (London: Hutchinson & Company, 1966), p. 15.

19. K. Reiskel, "Skatologische Inschriften," *Anthropophyteia,* 6 (1906), 245.

20. Renatus Hartogs, *Four-Letter Word Games* (New York: Dell Publishing Company, 1967), pp. 50-53.

21. Lee Sechrest and A. K. Olson, "Graffiti in Four Types of Institutions of Higher Education," *Journal of Sex Research,* 7 (1971), 62-71.

22. Hartogs, *Four-Letter Word Games,* p. 53.

8 TEAROOM TRADE

The excessive interest that graffiti focus on the size of the male penis often contains more than one theme. The first theme, as we noted in the previous chapter, is reassurance that one has not been castrated. In describing himself as the proud possessor of a remarkable organ, the writer is assuring himself that he is indeed a man and that his genital has not been severed. The second theme observable in these graffiti is patently homosexual. This is particularly evident in those graffiti that omit any reference to women:

I want to suck your dick.

My cock is only 10 inches long, so if anyone would like to suck meet here at 9 pm at any night[1]

I like to have sailors and truck drivers piss in my mouth

Please let me waddle up next to you caressing that hot load while slipping my bulging cock up your inviting asshole

I want a dick up my ass or one to suck

> I want to be fucked hard in the ass until I
> bleed. I will pay $15. I live off campus. Leave
> your name and address.
>
> How does it feel to get screwed in the ass
> and get a dick in your mouth? If you can help
> me tell me where to meet you.

The sheer bulk of these homosexual inscriptions has been noted and commented on by several authors. Of course there is no way of knowing whether these graffiti are written by homosexuals, but their homosexual nature is undeniably clear.

According to a remarkable sociological study by Laud Humphreys,[2] there is a direct relationship between the type of graffiti found in a particular toilet and the frequency of its usage by homosexuals. "The type of graffiti found does correlate with use of the room for homosexual purposes," declares Humphreys. "In the more active tearooms (toilets frequented by homosexuals for purposes of sex acts), I have often noticed inscriptions such as 'show hard—get sucked,' 'will suck cocks—10/12/66—all morning,' or 'I have 8 inches—who wants it?' "[3]

In documenting his study of the tearoom Humphreys gives the gist of an interview he had with a homosexual who made a point of coming to these toilets for the purpose of sex. According to this informant, "the presence of recent markings such as these reassures him that he has come to the right place for action." Writes Humphrey:

> homosexual locales are conspicuously lack-
> ing in initials, sketches of nude females, po-
> etry, and certain of the more classic four-
> letter words. Writing on the walls of the

true tearooms are straightforward, functional messages, lacking the fantasy content of the graffiti in most men's rooms."[4]

W. J. Gadpaille, a Denver psychiatrist, concurs with Humphreys that homosexuals utilize certain toilets for their impersonal rendezvous and that they often discover such places through the advertisements on the wall. Gadpaille claims that his homosexual patients have told him that they have acted on these invitations and that in some cases, these inscriptions have resulted in sexual encounters.[5]

Evidently, graffiti such as those that state the dimensions of the writer's penis or his desires and give a telephone number or an address may be much more than an outlet for psychological conflict. As noted by Humphreys and Gadpaille, these announcements may indeed be functional invitations to certain people who are on the lookout for suitable partners and places in what Humphreys has identified as the "tearoom trade."

Most of these homosexual graffiti are not meant to be acted upon, of course, but the fact is that by far the most frequent theme in graffiti deals with some aspect of homosexuality. This observation was first documented by Kinsey in 1953.[6] Kinsey counted the number of sexual graffiti in male toilets and found that the ratio of homosexual to heterosexual inscriptions was about 75 percent to 21 percent. Kinsey suggested that most of these homosexual graffiti were probably written by men who were not aware of the homosexual nature of their inscriptions but, nevertheless, harbored unsatisfied homosexual desires in their psyche.

Likewise arguing that graffiti reflect psychological conflict, Sechrest and his colleague at the University of the Philippines, Luis Flores, compared the lavatory inscriptions from the United States and the Philippines in terms of how often homosexual themes appeared in the graffiti from either area.[7] Sechrest and Flores decided to make such a comparison because of the contrast in the attitudes of these two cultures toward homosexuality: In the United States most Americans frown upon homosexual behavior; in the Philippines homosexuality is not uncommon, and the people are not very concerned about it.

To gather material for their study Sechrest and Flores scoured the toilets in twelve universities, five railway terminals, fifty restaurants and bars, and six miscellaneous locations in the United States, mainly around the Chicago area, and a comparable number of locations in the Philippines.

When the psychologists compared the graffiti from these two cultures, they found that whereas heterosexual graffiti occurred with about the same frequency in both cultures (about 13 percent in each), 42 percent of the American inscriptions were homosexual in content compared with only 2 percent from the Philippines. Sechrest and Flores concluded, therefore, that the highly significant difference in the proportion of homosexual graffiti in the United States reflects the difference in the extent of conflict over homosexual behavior in the two cultures. The lower incidence of such graffiti in the Philippines indicates that Filipinos are not too preoccupied with homosexuality—it is a fact of life for them, and they are not very bothered by that fact. Americans, however, experience a great deal of psychological conflict over homosexuality. Twenty-two percent of the American inscriptions found by Sechrest and Flores were invitations or requests for homosexual encounters. While clearly all were not meant to be acted upon, these graffiti probably represent wish fulfillments on the part of the writers.

Sechrest and Flores also noted that whereas both the American and Filipino graffiti contained drawings of male genitals, in the case of the Filipino graffiti the male organs were always drawn along with female genitalia, whereas the American drawings typically stood alone and "were explicitly expressions of homosexual fantasies or . . . were explicitly intended to arouse such fantasies in others."

In commenting on their findings, Sechrest and Flores suggest that while many of the graffiti they gathered were written by "normal" males, the fact that they were written at all indicates that the writers were preoccupied by this form of sexual behavior. "We are inclined to believe that it is conflict that leads to homosexual toilet wall inscriptions," they concluded from their study. In other words, although the producers of these graffiti are "normal," they harbor deep-rooted desires to initiate and participate in a homosexual relationship. The average Filipino male is far less concerned about being homosexual, and therefore he feels no need to talk or write about his feelings on the walls.

In a second study,[8] Sechrest and another colleague, A. Kenneth Olson, used graffiti to test Kinsey's finding that college students from lower socioeconomic backgrounds are less interested or stimulated by homosexual material than are male college students from higher socioeconomic backgrounds. The test involved comparing the graffiti from toilets in four different kinds of educational institutions: trade schools, junior colleges, four-year colleges, and professional schools (medicine, law, dentistry). The assumption behind this study was that these institutions attract the majority of their students from distinct socioeconomic backgrounds and therefore the graffiti from each school ought to reveal something about what kinds of conflicts the students in each setting experience.

The psychologists essentially corroborated Kinsey's earlier results. The incidence of heterosexual inscriptions was greater in the trade and junior colleges than in the four-year and professional schools. Conversely, the lowest incidence of homosexual inscriptions was found in the trade schools (4 percent) compared with 31 to 39 percent in the other three schools.

With respect to the nature of these homosexual inscriptions, Sechrest and Olson found that nearly all consisted of invitations and solicitations or of drawings of male genitalia. While Sechrest once more points out that such findings are not necessarily representative of the incidence of homosexual behavior in these schools, he contends that they probably do reflect the preoccupations and interests of the students who attend these institutions of higher learning.

Following Sechrest and Olson's lead, Terrance Stocker decided to examine the graffiti at some four-year and professional universities considered to be either conservative or liberal in their attitudes.[9] He chose Southern Illinois University at Carbondale as his liberal college and Eastern Kentucky University, at Bowling Green, as the conservative campus. He then collected graffiti from the toilets of each institution and compared them for their homosexual content.

Approximately 26 percent of the inscriptions at the conservative campus were found to contain a homosexual theme compared with approximately 14 percent at the liberal campus. As in the Sechrest and Flores study, Stocker pointed out that the more liberal the campus, the less the conflict concerning homosexuality and therefore the fewer wall inscriptions dealing with this theme.[10]

Stocker has also noted that the gay liberation movement has been responsible for changing American attitudes concerning homosexuality, and he has pointed
out that this change is reflected in the graffiti of the
past twenty-five years. For instance, there has been a
considerable decrease from 1953, when Kinsey found
that 75 percent of the graffiti written by American
males was homosexual in content. In 1966 Sechrest
and Flores found about 42 percent of their American
graffiti contained a homosexual theme. By 1971 this
proportion had dropped to 36 percent according to
Sechrest and Olson. By 1972 Stocker found the over-
all proportion of such graffiti to be only about 16 percent. On the basis of this decline, Stocker predicts
that "within five to ten years homosexual graffiti on
the college campus will be nonexistent."

Studies such as these represent an interesting example of how graffiti can be used to gain insight into
the changing cultural mores of a society. By examining
the themes present in graffiti, the social scientist can
attempt to understand what the individual writer has
in mind and, by extension, what society as a whole is
preoccupied with. The more frequently a theme is evident, the more likely the idea contained in that theme
is shared by a group. The changes in the frequency
with which a theme is expressed over the years also
tell the social scientist how the attitudes toward the
behavior represented by that theme have changed.
Graffiti can thus be a valuable tool in illuminating our
changing society. As pointed out by many other
authors, graffiti may be the only unbiased tool available to future generations for understanding past
generations.

NOTES

1. A. W. Read, *Lexical Evidence from Folk Epigraphy in Western North America* (Paris: Privately published, 1935), p. 20.

2. Laud Humphreys, *Tearoom Trade* (Chicago: Aldine Publishing Company, 1970).

3. Ibid., p. 72.

4. Ibid., p. 73.

5. W. J. Gadpaille, "Graffiti: Its Psychodynamic Significance." *Sexual Behavior* 2 (1971), 48.

6. Alfred C. Kinsey, *Sex in the Human Female* (Philadelphia: W. B. Saunders Company, 1953).

7. Lee Sechrest and Luis Flores, "Homosexuality in the Philippines and the United States: The Handwriting on the Wall," *Journal of Social Psychology,* 79 (1969), 3-12.

8. Lee Sechrest and A. Kenneth Olson, "Graffiti in Four Types of Institutions of Higher Education," *Journal of Sex Research,* 1 (1971), 62-71.

9. T. L. Stocker, L. W. Dutcher, S. M. Hargrove, and E. A. Cook, "Social Analysis of Graffiti," *Journal of American Folklore,* 85 (1972), 356-366.

10. For a diametrically opposed interpretation, see G. Gonos, V. Mulkern, and N. Poushinsky, "Anonymous Expression: A Structural View of Graffiti," *Journal of American Folklore,* 82 (1976), 40-48.

9 AGGRESSIVELY SEXUAL GRAFFITI

One of the most frequently encountered verbal expressions of anger in American culture is "fuck you!" an expletive that carries with it the threat of impending sexual assault. The fact that expressions of anger such as this often take the language of sex is seemingly a rather puzzling state of affairs, since sex is usually thought of as being a part of love, not hate.

The puzzle ceases to exist, however, when we realize that there is a direct biological relationship between aggression and sex. For example, it has long been known to farmers and zoologists that castration renders aggressive males quite docile. This is because the testes produce a hormone called testosterone, which is responsible for the male's masculinity. With the removal of the testes and therefore the source of testosterone, the behavioral characteristics that we associate with the male sex are soon diminished if not entirely lost. Injection of this male hormone back into castrated male animals, however, will completely reinstate their previously aggressive behavior.

Animals likewise do not fight very much until they reach the age of puberty. This is because no testosterone is produced by the testes prior to this stage in their development. On the other hand, if these juvenile animals are injected with testosterone, they will begin to fight before they reach puberty. In monkeys, a species closely related to man, electrical stimulation of certain parts of the brain has been observed to elicit penile erection. Very near these same areas in the brain is a center that causes the animal to act with rage and aggression when it is stimulated.[1]

With respect to human beings, there is also a large amount of psychological evidence indicating an interesting relationship between aggression and sex. In one such study the level of hostility in a classroom of college students was increased by having their instructor belittle them.[2] Following his insulting remarks, the instructor asked the students to participate in a test in which he gave them directions in an arrogant tone. The test consisted of the students having to make up short stories about ambiguous-looking pictures.

In the control condition a similar group of students was asked to write stories about the same pictures, but these students were not previously subjected to the insults and arrogance shown to the other group. When the answers of the students in these two groups were analyzed by judges who were unaware of which treatment had been given to whom, it was found that the students experiencing the insults were more likely to incorporate aggressive and sexual ideas into their stories than were the students in the control group. The fact that the formers' stories showed greater hostility is to be expected from the kind of treatment given them. Why this hostility also produced an increase in sexual fantasy is not so readily understandable.

Another experiment of this kind involved introducing students at the University of Minnesota to an individual supposedly from a prestigious Ivy League college who had come to Minnesota for the purpose of conducting some studies.[3] The newcomer immediately set out to antagonize the students by telling them that the task they were being asked to participate in had been simplified to conform to the inferior type of student that attended a place like the University of Minnesota.

Ambiguous pictures were administered to these students, and their stories were compared with those produced by another group of students that had not been previously treated in this derogatory manner. Again the psychologists found that when the students were angered, there was an increase in the aggressiveness and sexual themes found in their stories.

On the basis of these and many other similar studies there now seems to be impressive evidence, both biological and psychological, for the curious relationship between sex and aggression in animals and humans. It is probably for this reason that in name calling or cursing, the speaker or writer very frequently describes the behavior or the appearance of his foe in terms that carry sexual connotations. Before examining this phenomenon specifically with regard to graffiti, let us consider one of the many factors that can lead to such behavior.

A classic hypothesis in psychology about the origins of aggressive behavior was proposed by John Dollard and Neal Miller in 1939 in a book entitled *Frustration and Aggression.* According to these investigators, frustration occurs whenever there is interference with some goal-directed behavior and this frustration tends to induce aggression by stimulating a motivational state such as anger. The occurrence of aggression is then seen as a form of catharsis in that it serves as an outlet for the release of this frustration-induced tension.

There are, of course, any of a number of different

ways that some thing or some person can prevent us from attaining our goals. The obstacle can be a physical one—a barrier or a fence, a long line ahead of us at a box office that threatens any moment to post a sold-out sign, or a traffic jam when we are in a hurry. However, it is only when we perceive that these obstacles have been knowingly and deliberately placed before us that they begin to induce frustration.

Less tangible but no less formidable an obstacle is prejudice. For instance, trying to date someone or trying to get a job but being turned down because we are the "wrong" religion or the "wrong" color can be extremely frustrating. Whether or not this frustration leads to overt aggression, however, depends upon a number of factors such as the fear of retaliation or punishment, opportunity, target, and the individual's own peculiar reaction pattern to frustration.

In general, physically aggressive behavior is not tolerated in Western society, especially when it is turned against figures of authority. The inhibitions preventing violence against individuals who are weak or who belong to minority groups are sometimes less formidable, but physical aggression is still not usually resorted to as a result of fear of eventual retaliation, punishment, or a guilty conscience.

There are other ways of causing distress besides physical violence. Words may be substituted for action. Moreover, it is often safer to swear at someone than hit him. Name calling is another example of such aggression. Humor, which we shall examine at greater length in a later chapter, has long been recognized as a vehicle for aggression.

In graffiti we have yet another outlet for the expression of hostile impulses. Although direct outbursts against someone are not funny, for some people "Hate can be enjoyable," as one graffito puts it. This enjoyment is in keeping with the cathartic function of aggression in the frustration-aggression hypothesis. This enjoyment of hate may account for graffiti that are venomous in content and that make no pretense at hiding their aggression:

> Watch out commies, liberals, niggers, jews, etc.

> My father was a captain in the SS. I wish we had some of his men to exterminate all people who support these goddamn minorities in this country.

These graffiti are examples of aggression against minority groups. More often than not, however, such prejudice is unrelated to personal experience with any particular group and depends instead on impersonal social factors. In all likelihood, the writers of these graffiti have had no direct contact with members of the groups they disparage but are merely venting their anger against what they feel is a condoned target for their particular subculture. They remain anonymous, however, so that there is no danger of retaliation or punishment.

We shall never know the circumstances or events that provoked most of these outbursts, but in some cases concern over sex appears to contribute at least partially to the attack:

> Two things I cannot tolerate: Niggers that date our white girls, and faggots (the perverted shit eaters)

> Sarah Goldberg will fuck any gentile . . . if he's circumcised

Do niggers dream about anything but white
cunt?

(underneath, different handwriting):

No because they dream in black and white

After seeing nigger women I can understand
why black niggers prefer white women

When aggression cannot be vented directly against
the frustrating agent, it will often be displaced onto a
substitute, a phenomenon called scapegoating. The
Nazis judiciously employed scapegoating when they
blamed the so-called Jewish conspiracy for Germany's
economic ills. By so doing, they were able to divert
the economic frustrations of the German people away
from the real problems confronting the nation and
onto a defenseless minority. The same kind of psychological phenomenon also appears to be evident in
graffiti such as those just cited wherein sexual frustrations appear to have been diverted from the frustrating agents (about which we know nothing) onto
the black person and the Jew.

At the beginning of this chapter we stated that the
expression "fuck you!" is actually a veiled threat of
sexual assault. This is more readily apparent in German, where the verb *ficken*, "to copulate," also means
"to strike."[4] In this regard, G. Legman has observed
that the penis is frequently looked upon as a weapon
in folklore. For every joke, limerick, or synonym for
the penis in which the pleasure of the woman is involved, says Legman, "ten jokes or limericks or syn-
onyms will be found in which the penis is used to harm,
impale, or, plainly, kill her."[5] Readers familiar with
Freud's *The Interpretation of Dreams* will also recall

how often the penis is symbolized in dreams as a weapon such as a gun or knife. Thus when we encounter variants of the "fuck you" graffito, such as "Fuck uptight niggers . . . signed Whitemen," we should be aware that in this verbal assault we have another instance of the way in which sex is closely associated with aggression in the human mind.

Less bitter, but equally offensive, are those graffiti that denigrate classes of people by associating them with excrement:

Eat shit, a million Polacks can't be wrong

Eat shit, a million niggers can't be wrong

Although we have no way of knowing for certain, we believe that the original upon which these two graffiti were based was this graffito: "Eat shit, a million flies can't be wrong," which in turn was originally based on the familiar saying, "Fifty million Frenchmen can't be wrong." By merely substituting the target for the word *flies*, the writer anonymously hurls his anger upon his perceived foes with impunity.

The fact that society generally regards excrement with disgust means that anything or anyone associated with it will share in that disgust. Hence one way to characterize a group or an individual as loathsome is to refer to them as "dirt":

If black is beautiful
I just shit a masterpiece

This graffito thus becomes a derisive thrust against the emergent black pride movement and its slogan, "Black is beautiful." In a similar vein is this exchange:

First writer: If they're not different—why
                did god make them black
                like shit?

Second writer: Why did he make you white
                like toilet paper?

Politically, the association of a candidate with "dirt"
may take the form:

When you wipe
Think of Reagan

When Senator Barry Goldwater of Arizona ran for the
presidency, in 1964, two graffiti directed at him took
their cue from his name:

When I look down, I see Goldwater

Urine is Goldwater; the only benefit is derived from the comfort of its removal

Richard Nixon too has been the brunt of many uncom-
plimentary graffiti during his career. Sometimes the
association is with excrement:

How can you Republicans shit when your
asshole is in Washington?

I came here to dump Nixon

And sometimes the emphasis is placed on sex rather
than on elimination:

Don't change dicks in the middle of a good
screw. Reelect Nixon in '72

Nixon's father did not know when to withdraw either

The latter example was popular at the height of the Vietnam conflict when more and more Americans were demanding an end to the fighting.

Referring to someone by a part of the sexual anatomy has much the same intent:

All shmucks are dicks
All dicks are shmucks
Nixon is a dick
Therefore he's a shmuck

Vote for Nixon, he's one dick that's up and coming

Still another device for bringing contumely down upon some person or group is to hurl the accusation of perverted sexual behavior:

Cubans are a funny bunch
What we call pussy
They call lunch

Get the dick out of the White House and into your mouth

It is fairly clear that all of these graffiti are essentially expressions of hostility, the function of which would appear to be that of "letting off steam." In the next chapter, we shall delve further into the problem of why such aggression takes the vocabulary of sex and excretion for its outlet.

NOTES

1. P. D. MacLean and D. W. Ploog, "Cerebral Representation of Penile Erection," *Journal of Neurophysiology*, 25 (1962), 29-55.

2. A. M. Barclay and R. N. Haber, "The Relation of Aggressive to Sexual Motivation," *Journal of Personality*, 37 (1969), 462-475.

3. R. A. Clark and M. R. Sensibar, "The Relationship Between Symbolic and Manifest Projections of Sexuality with Some Incidental Correlates," *Journal of Abnormal and Social Psychology*, 56 (1955), 327-334.

4. See Chapter 1, note 25.

5. G. Legman, *Rationale of the Dirty Joke* (London: Panther Books, 1969), p. 295.

10 THE ROLE OF HUMOR IN GRAFFITI

Humor is where you find it and some of the best humor in America today is found on public toilet walls. This is the reason that so many people are curious about what the walls have to say—they want to be in on the joke.

The fact that graffiti are read for their humor is explicitly stated by this graffitist as he makes a joke of his own:

Listen buddy, the joke's not up
here on the wall . . .
It's in your hand

Students of humor have long recognized that while the desire to be funny may be the obvious motivation behind joking, some inner conflict often determines what one tries to be funny about. Thus Legman, author of the now classic and encyclopedic *Rationale of the Dirty Joke*, points out: "It may be stated axiomatically that a person's favorite joke is the key to that person's character."[1]

The most penetrating analysis of the function of laughter in society is Freud's monumental *Jokes and Their Relation to the Unconscious*. In Freud's opinion the main reason people tell jokes is so that they can achieve pleasure by symbolically gratifying basic impulses not allowed free expression by society. Ordinarily, these impulses are inhibited because the individual has learned from past experience that direct expression of them is not generally approved. As a result, conflict is created within the individual between the desire to express these impulses and the internalized restraints that keep him from doing so.

To achieve the innate pleasure that Freud associates with the expression of such forbidden actions, he argues that it is necessary for the impulses to assume some disguise in order to circumvent the internalized standards of censorship. One such disguise is the joke.

Jokes make us laugh, Freud contends, when pent-up psychic energy is released without causing guilt or conflict. The more energy released, the louder the "belly laugh." However, since "no one can be content with having made a joke for himself alone," jokes are made public, either verbally or by writing them somewhere such as in a book or on a wall where they will be read by others.

The laughter generated by jokes gives pleasure in two ways: (1) by serving as an escape hatch for the impulse and (2) by serving as an outlet for the anxiety associated with repressing that impulse.

Jokes, it has frequently been noted, are one of the most characteristic and least offensive ways of discharging aggression. The wish to cause someone else harm is typically held in check or repressed. Direct expression of aggression is not very funny. For laughter to occur, aggression must be aroused, repressed, and allowed to escape. For the latter to happen, the aggressive impulse must be disguised, and one such disguise is the joke.

The humor in a joke depends on the cleverness of

the disguise. The individual who makes up what he believes is a clever joke tries the disguise out on someone else. The listener or reader recognizes the hostility as well as the disguise. The joke causes him to feel an aggressive impulse, and by laughing he allows the psychic energy associated with that impulse to be released.

The part played by humor in the regulation of socially unacceptable behavior has also been the object of some attention by anthropologists. Levine, for instance, has observed that even among the most Victorian-minded tribes of American Indians, violation of nearly every social taboo, including incest, occurs with impunity by those who adopt the role of the clown during certain festivals. Using this ancient disguise of humor, the Indian may regress to the nadir or climb to the apogee of the inviolate, without the least social restraint.[2]

The only requirement for enjoyment of a joke is that the audience be in some sort of psychological empathy with the jokester. Both must share the same basic thoughts and impulses and the same inhibitory pressures preventing their direct expression. It is for this reason that jokes that are funny to people of some nationalities are not funny to others of a different national origin. Coming from different cultural backgrounds, people simply do not share all of the same psychological dispositions. The same is also true of people coming from different subcultures.

This subculture factor is nicely illustrated in an experiment in which Jews and gentiles were asked to rate the humor in a number of jokes, some of which were not very complimentary to Jews. It was found that whereas the jokes containing no ethnic, religious, or racial overtones were judged equally funny by both groups, when the jokes dealt with Jewish themes in a disparaging fashion, they were rated as being significantly funnier by gentile students.

In a related study, psychologists asked male and female students to judge a number of jokes in which the brunt of the humor was either maleness or femaleness. The results showed that men judged the anti-female jokes funnier than did women and vice versa in the case of the antimale jokes.

One prediction that might be made on the basis of this notion of psychological disposition is that people who are made angry ought to appreciate jokes that contain hostility, much more than would complacent individuals. Similarly, sexually aroused people should appreciate humor containing a sexual theme to a greater extent than people who are not sexually aroused.

Such an experiment was conducted by J. F. Strickland: College students were assigned at random to one of three conditions.[3] In the hostile condition the experimenter attempted to make the students angry by being curt toward them and by making them wait alone in a room containing nothing but a table and chair. No apologies were given, nor was there any explanation of the delay, and immediately upon the return of the experimenter the humor test was administered. In the sexual condition, the students were shown photographs of nude models and were told that they were to rate them on the basis of sexual attractiveness. Immediately thereafter the humor test was administered. In the control condition the humor test was administered soon after the students entered the experimental room. In each of the conditions the students were tested individually.

The humor test itself consisted of a number of cartoons that had previously been judged by several impartial judges to contain either aggressive, sexual, or nonsensical themes. When he analyzed the test answers, Strickland found that the students in the hostile condition rated those cartoons that contained a hostile theme as being the funniest. Similarly, students in the sex condition group rated cartoons that had a sexual theme as the funniest. The control group likewise rated the sexual cartoons as being funniest, but they derived less pleasure from these cartoons than did the sex condition group.

These findings thus demonstrate the importance of the individual's own disposition or psychological set as a factor in the appreciation of humor. A hostile disposition increases one's receptivity to jokes of a hostile nature; sexual arousal predisposes one to an appreciation of jokes that deal with sex.

A somewhat similar kind of experiment was conducted by Dworkin and Efran, who also found that increasing a person's hostility made him respond more appreciatively to humor containing hostility than toward humor in general.[4] Dworkin and Efran also found, however, that listening to a joke, whatever its nature, decreased an individual's feelings of hostility. In other words, they were able to demonstrate an important aspect of humor in an experimental setting, namely, that humor has a way of dissipating resentment innocuously.

Thus jokes that contain some kind of insult are only funny because both the teller and the listener recognize the aggression inherent in the joke. When the joke includes some topic about which both also feel some anxiety, they are doubly funny. Hence jokes that include some sexual element have a ready audience of potential laughers. The same is true of jokes that are scatological.

One of the main types of humor as it is found in graffiti involves the exploitation of an individual or a group through the double meaning of words. The jokester says something. Unbeknown to the listener, there is some ambiguity in what has been said, and the jokester then transforms the original message. By transforming the meaning, the jokester has put one over on the listener. Recognizing that he has been deceived, the listener is amused. We have already seen some examples of this transformation technique in the previous chapter, for example: "Don't change dicks in the middle of a good screw. Reelect Nixon in '72."

In the first exhortation we visualize "penis" when we come to the word *dicks*, especially in the context of the word *screw*. The second exhortation, however, shows us that *dicks* is really a reference to Dick Nixon, and *screw* is a reflection of the writer's dissatisfaction with the President's administration. In this example the jokester has fooled his readers and in the process has attacked the President. In so doing he has also engaged in a thought (assaulting the President of the United States) that might otherwise have been subject to internalized inhibitions. The reader is also amused because he has been harmlessly led into thinking of the obvious meaning, only to be fooled by the second sense of the words.

In the following example of another play on words, Nixon is again the brunt of the graffiti writer's humor: "President Nixon has one thing in common with a rubber. They both give you a feeling of confidence while you're being screwed."

Readers of graffiti are equally capable of manipulating thoughts expressed on toilet walls, especially when they do not wish to acknowledge the psychological implications of the messages they read. For example, consider this exchange:

First writer: My mother made me a homo-
                     sexual

Second writer: If I sent her the wool, would
                    she make me one too.

This particular transformation has previously been
discussed by Martin Grotjahn, a psychiatrist who is
well known for his penetrating studies of what makes
people laugh. Grotjahn points out that the first half of
this joke alerts the reader who identifies with the
writer and becomes anxious at the prospect of the
emasculating mother. The reader has thus "intro-
jected" the image of homosexuality, and it bothers
him to think of himself in this fashion.

In the second half of the joke the anxiety is dis-
pelled. The disguise is recognized and appreciated,
and pleasure is felt. The sudden release of repressed
psychic energy associated with the thought of being
homosexual, combined with the infantile amusement
of playing with words (feces), all give rise to laughter.[5]

The same kind of analysis could also be made of
this exchange:

First writer: I've got what every woman
                     wants

Second writer: You must be in the fur coat
                    business

Here the first writer is referring to and bragging about
his genital. The reader visualizes a sizable male organ
and probably feels that his own is inferior by comparison (see Chapter 7). This is a psychically painful
admission because he may equate penis size with
masculinity, and therefore the less impressive his

penis, the less of a man he is. The second half of the exchange allows him to discharge his pent-up emotions in laughter, since what every woman wants is not a penis but a fur coat. His masculinity is not in doubt, and he has turned the tables on the first writer.

In the same vein, we should not omit this now classic exchange:

> First writer: I'm 11″ long and 5″ wide
>
> Second writer: Fine, but how big's your prick?

Here is another, but less clever, manipulation:

> One of the most underestimated things in the world is a good shit

(Underneath in different hand writing):

> It's about time someone said something nice about a dental student.

And here is a final example:

> First writer: The level of graffiti in here is appalling. Apparently most med students have spent so much time in labs that most of their brain has become clogged with chemicals, either come up with something original or I'll shit elsewhere.

Second writer: A lot of undergrads and pharmacy students study in here too, you know

Third writer: Why don't they come on out and study in the carrels like the rest of us do?

Here we have an initial lament that the graffiti in the medical school library toilet is unoriginal. The first writer accuses the medical students of being brain damaged and threatens not to return if no improvements are forthcoming in the quality of the graffiti. His threat, incidently, indicates he is an individual who sets great store on his waste. His statement is read by a second individual who feels the attack personally, since he focuses his attention on the accusation rather than on the threat. This person is either a medical student defending himself and his colleagues or a student from some other faculty who feels that he has been insulted in not being numbered among those who make use of the library. The third writer cares nothing for the first writer's accusation or threat. His only interest is in humiliating the second writer by making it seem that undergraduates and pharmacy students are peculiar individuals, since they choose to study in the toilet instead of the library itself as do most people. This twisting of the second writer's intentions causes us to laugh. The second writer is made to appear ridiculous in the process. This is the laughter of hostility, attack, and aggression. In his humiliation the second writer is made to appear pitiful.

Not all graffiti that are funny are hostile, of course, but whenever a graffito derogates some individual or group, or dwells upon their rejection, humiliation, incapacitation, suffering, or destruction, then we may be fairly certain that we are dealing with a veiled form of aggression. Hertzler puts it this way:

> aggressive, sardonic, satirical, or otherwise, hostile laughter is also a mechanism widely and purposely resorted to in order to oppose other persons, or the behavior of other persons or groups. . . . It is used as a means of carrying on conflict, as a weapon for attacking, thwarting and hurting those against whom it is directed individually or collectively. . . . Men have long known that if they can make any man or group or concept or belief or social movement an object of derisive laughter, he or it is weakened and possibly doomed to failure.[6]

It is in this light that the following graffito must be regarded:

> If black is beautiful
> I just shit a masterpiece

On humor such as this, Burma has written:

> throughout this history of minority-majority group relations in this country the set of techniques which we may denominate by the general term humor has played a definite role in interpersonal and inter-group relationships. Apparently all minority groups suffer derogation in this manner, and apparently all use the same weapon in return.[7]

Of course, graffiti can be statements of aggression without being funny. But the process of socialization has taught some people to inhibit direct signs of hostility. By resorting to humor, however, this aggression can still be expressed. Hostile humor, observes Hertzler,

> has the advantage of permitting us to make our enemy appear ridiculous or to confound his strategy without resort to outright verbal or physical attack. It can also be shrewdly used to exercise aggression or malice in situations where the actors are unable to engage in these openly and directly because of law, moral codes, or conventions, as in attacking marriage or the church.[8]

As Hertzler points out, not only may individuals and groups be the brunt of hostile humor, institutions and concepts can also be attacked. One institution that frequently comes under fire is the church as is evident in these inscriptions:

> God is dead
> But don't worry, Mary's pregnant again
>
> Christmas cancelled . . . Joseph confessed
>
> Easter will be postponed this year . . . they found the body
>
> Come home Judas . . . all is forgiven

Here the miracles of the New Testament and the treatment of Judas are centered out for attention. The writers of these sentiments are poking fun at something they can no longer believe in. In the more materialistic world of today these writers find the tenets of the church no longer acceptable or relevant.

The personage of Jesus has become the brunt of graffiti humor:

> Jesus saves . . . Moses invests

> First writer: Jesus saves

> Second writer: He must make more than I do

> Jesus was a mother fucker

> Jesus had an Edipussy complex

And God may be dead, but not in graffiti:

> God is dead
>   —Signed Nietzsche

(Underneath):

> Nietzsche is dead
>   —Signed God

> God is not dead, he's hiding in the Amazon

> God is not dead, he just doesn't want to get involved

The clergy has also been attacked in graffiti:

> Said the priest to the girl
> I'll stick my pole
> In your dirty old hole
> Now work your ass
> To save your soul
>   (From Read)

By means of laughter, then, the graffiti writer is able to alleviate certain feelings of anxiety he may be harboring. The disguise of humor allows normally forbidden impulses or thoughts to escape what Freud has called the censor, and the more clever the disguise, the more pleasure it arouses.

This goal of getting pleasure is motive enough for the ordinary joke, but when humor also enables the jokester to give vent openly to that which is normally inhibited, then the pleasure is doubly satisfactory. But there is also the possibility that the graffiti writer may be unwilling to admit even to himself that he harbors the kinds of thoughts he writes about. Then humor is once again a useful social device, since the jokester is able to deny his impulses by claiming that his intention is only to make someone else laugh.

On this point of self-denial, Legman has observed that

> the folktale or joke . . . represents a protective mechanism whereby the seriousness, and even the physical reality, of the situation can be denied and made light of, by telling it —or accepting some serious original anecdote describing it simply as a joke; as something allowing the accumulated tension of living this situation, or telling about it, or listening to it, to relieve itself harmlessly by the necessary explosion of laughter.[9]

NOTES

1. G. Legman, *Rationale of the Dirty Joke*, (London: Panther Books, 1969), p. 16.

2. S. Levine, "Regression in Primitive Clowning," *Psychoanalytic Quarterly,* 30 (1961), 72-83.

3. J. F. Strickland, "The Effect of Motivation Arousal on Human Preferences," *Journal of Abnormal and Social Psychology,* 59 (1959), 278-281.

4. E. S. Dworkin and J. S. Efran, "The Angered: Their Susceptibility to Varieties of Humor," *Journal of Personality and Social Psychology,* 6 (1967), 233-236.

5. Martin Grotjahn, "Smoking, Coughing, Laughing and Applause: A Comparative Study of Respiratory Symbolism," *International Journal of Psychoanalysis*, 53 (1972), 345-349.

6. J. O. Hertzler, *Laughter,* (New York: Exposition Press, 1970), p. 87.

7. J. J. Burma, "Humor as a Technique in Race Conflict," *American Sociological Review*, 22 (1957), 107-110.

8. Ibid.

9. Legman, *Rationale*, p. 18.

11 MISCELLANEOUS SEXUAL THOUGHTS EXPRESSED THROUGH GRAFFITI

As previously mentioned, a number of sexual behaviors are considered unnatural because they do not lead to procreation. One of the most deeply rooted of these so-called unnatural acts is bestiality, intercourse between humans and animals.

What is considered unnatural in one society, as we have often noted, may be perfectly natural in another. A once popular maxim among devout Arabs, for example, was that "The pilgrimage to Mecca is not perfected save by copulation with a camel." Bestiality was also not uncommon among religious Hindus. Among the latter, priests used to urge the devout to copulate with cattle or monkeys, both of which are sacred to the Hindu religion.

The ancient Romans were known for their love of mass spectacles, such as gladiatorial combat and the periodic mauling and devouring of Christians by lions. Another popular diversion was watching animals have intercourse with women, via either the vagina or the anus. The animals (dogs, horses, bulls, giraffes, and so on) were not only taught to copulate with women, but they were also instructed how to rape any female who did not willingly submit.

Bestiality is presently condemned in nearly all societies and violation can be legally punished with imprisonment for many years. But the idea still fascinates some people as illustrated by these graffiti:

Little mother Hubbard
Went to the cupboard
To get Rover a bone.
When she bent over,
Old Rover, he drove her
And she realized he had one of his own

Mary had a little lamb
She took the sheep to sleep
The sheep turned out to be a ram
Mary had a little lamb

There was a young girl from the park
who blew dead bears after dark
When she was asked why
she said with a sigh
I guess because it's a lark

A cunt's a cunt
Even on a cow[1]

Montana—where men are men and women are sheep[2]

However, the fascination produced at the thought of an animal committing bestiality with a woman stems not from the coupling of two different species, but rather from the identification of the animal with the writers of such graffiti. The dog who drove the old lady or the ram that slept with Mary is not a dog or ram at all; the animals represent men, and these graffiti symbolize a deep-seated desire on the part of these men to commit rape, not bestiality. The writers of these graffiti are instilling the animals with their own fantasies.

In the case of those graffiti that seemingly are direct expressions of bestial fantasies, there is a latent component inherent in these themes that should also be mentioned. This is especially true in the case of those inscriptions that juxtapose the male with a female animal such as a cow. The latter is a centuries' old symbol for motherhood with respect to the milk-giving capacity of these animals; hence the graffito that acknowledges that cows are females may in fact be disguised Oedipal wishes.

Fellatio and cunnilingus are oral-genital sexual contacts that are also rigidly tabooed in Western society, but like other "unnatural" acts, this is not a universal taboo. The most famous fellatrice, the name given to a woman who performs fellatio, was Queen Cleopatra of Egypt. Reputed to have fellated a hundred Roman noblemen during one night's orgy, she was heralded throughout the ancient world by many names, one of which was "the ten-thousand mouthed woman."[3]

In China Empress Wu Hu, one of the world's earliest feminists, regarded fellatio as degrading to women. To demonstrate her superiority over men she required all court personnel and visiting statesmen to display their official obeisance to her imperial personage by performing cunnilingus upon her, a fact preserved in paintings showing her standing with an open robe while some visitor kneels before her and licks her genitals.[4]

We have already seen that fellatio, the exhortation to "suck" is a common theme in homosexual graffiti. Other examples of this type are: "Get the dick out of the White House and into your mouth," which capitalizes on the dual meaning of the word *dick* to evoke laughter and thus assuage the anxiety surrounding fellatio. In the case of heterosexual preoccupation with oral-genital sex, we have the following:

> Observe national cunnilingus week, take a clitoris to lunch

> I would like to fuck and eat some girl

> I eat pussy

> If Miles Standish had shot a cat instead of a turkey we would all be eating pussy Thanks-giving[5]

> There was a young girl from Sublime
> Who would blow at the drop of a dime
> She's drop to her knees
> And then puff and wheeze
> Till you asked her to stop for a time

> Here's to the girl with the coal black eyes
> The soul of deceet the inventor of lies
> I hope in hell she will roost
> She sucked my dick with a hell of a dose[6]

The prospect of venereal disease is something hardly welcomed, and it too preoccupies the minds of certain people:

> V.D. is nothing to clap about

> Here I lay my Celia down
> I got the pox and she got half a crown[7]

Crude though they may be, these inscriptions represent the preoccupations and possible obsessions of a larger percentage of Americans than is commonly realized. "The males who make the inscriptions, and the males who read them," Kinsey wrote over a quarter of a century ago, "are exposing their unsatisfied desires. The inscriptions portray what they would like to experience in real life."[8]

The fact that these preoccupations are so prevalent, as graffiti seem to indicate they are, seems to indicate that our society, with its rigid taboos on certain sexual behaviors, is causing a great many people to feel distressed psychologically.

Sexologists have repeatedly stressed that the kinds of sexual behavior that are tabooed in one society may be perfectly acceptable in another. Homosexuality, for instance, is frowned upon in the United States, but in the Philippines, as we have seen, it is quite common. Consequently, the theme of homosexuality frequently enters into American graffiti but this is rarely the case among Filipinos. Similarly, in Western countries polygyny is rare; in the Arab countries it is a way of life. Although not discussed as such in America, promiscuity is likewise a popular though veiled theme in American graffiti.

Is there any way of determining what should be regarded as natural and what as unnatural sexual behavior? Earlier we said that sexual behavior that leads to procreation is generally considered natural and that which does not is looked upon as being unnatural. Noted sexologist Albert Ellis has drawn attention to the incongruity of such a criterion.[9]

While the sex drive is important in determining the frequency of sexual behavior, Ellis points out that this drive is capable of being held in check. The expression of this drive, whether it be homosexual or heterosexual, is primarily dependent upon the culture one lives in. Therefore, what is natural for one society may not be so for another. For this reason, some biologists have argued that the only absolute criterion for defining what is a natural and therefore an acceptable form of sexual activity is that which is based on the concept of procreation. Such a criterion would thus exclude homosexuality, masturbation, oral-genital contacts, and so on, from the realm of natural sexual acts. However, if carried to its logical extreme, Ellis points out that such a code would permit premarital sex and adultery if engaged in without any attempt at contraception. Furthermore, all methods of contraception would likewise not be permissible.

The absurdity of such a state of affairs clearly indicates that there is no biological criterion for defining what is natural in sex. Societies impose such codes arbitrarily, and they must be prepared to accept the responsibility for what these codes do to people. The psychological problems—conflicts, guilt feelings, shame, anxiety—associated with violation of these codes, evident in graffiti, are very real and must be seen as originating not from the sex drives themselves but from the social attitudes toward sex.

NOTES

1. A. W. Read, *Lexical Evidence from Folk Epigraphy in Western North America* (Paris: Privately published, 1935), p. 48.

2. R. Reisner, *Graffiti: Two Thousand Years of Wall Writing* (New York: Cowles Book Company, 1971), p. 41.

3. G. L. Simons, *Simon's Book of World Sexual Records* (New York: Pyramid Books, 1975), p. 140.

4. Ibid.

5. Reisner, *Graffiti,* p. 38.

6. Read, *Lexical Evidence,* p. 49.

7. Hurlo Thrumbo, *The Merry-Thought or, the Glass-Window Bog-House Miscellany* (London: Privately published, 1731), p. 14.

8. Alfred C. Kinsey, *Sex in the Human Female* (Philadelphia: W. B. Saunders Company, 1953), p. 675.

9. Albert Ellis, "What Is Normal Sex Behavior?" in M. F. Demartina (ed.), *Sexual Behavior and Personality Characteristics* (New York: Grove Press, 1963), pp. 19-30.

12 FEMALE GRAFFITI

Female graffiti, according to Lomas and Welt-man, are "sparse and unimaginative." Sechrest and Flores, who are of the same opinion, note that "collecting data from female conveniences is wearing and frustrating. Some of the most likely looking places prove totally barren."[1]

Explanations for the paucity of female graffiti range from sexist statements to the effect that "females are less inclined to make wall inscriptions of any sort, and less inclined to make erotic wall inscriptions, because of their greater regard for the moral codes and the social conventions" (Kinsey),[2] to observations such as "females are, in this low artistic medium as little productive as they have long been noted to be in the higher forms such as music, literature and painting" (Sechrest and Flores).[3] This latter observation, incidently, is echoed by a female graffiti writer herself: "Do you realize that there has never been a great female composer and only 2 or 3 artists?"

Eugene Landy and John Steele of the University of Oklahoma's Institute for Group Relations have likewise noted the paucity of female graffiti, but they contend that women find different outlets for the pressures they feel than do men. Landy and Steele point out, for example, that there is a greater incidence of smoking in female restrooms than in male conveniences as indicated by the number of ashtrays and cigarette butts found in each. On the basis of such evidence, they suggest that smoking is the female substitute for the graffiti of the male: "Whereas males act out this need (to give vent to their inner feelings) by creating graffiti, females smoke it out."[4]

L. Rudin and M. Harles concur with this idea. They too have remarked that women smoke in restrooms to a greater extent than do men. Female graffiti, they have found, only occur in quantity where there is no smoking lounge in the women's restroom.[5] And Luana Martilla, a female graffitiologist from Berkeley, California, contends that females write fewer graffiti than males because there are "cultural factors which inhibit women from engaging in aggressive or defiant acts," which she feels graffiti represent.[6]

Yet another explanation is a fanciful flight of the mind called the pregnancy envy hypothesis. This hypothesis has been proposed by Dundes, whom we previously encountered in connection with his idea that graffiti writing represents a "primitive smearing impulse."[7]

In discussing the differences in male-female graffiti, Dundes has come up with a rather novel explanation. He has argued that men write graffiti as a symbolic surrogate for their inability to produce babies. "In essence," Dundes argues, "men are envious of women's ability to bear children and they seek to find various substitute gratifications. . . ." Having no need of such substitutions, women are thus less prone to writing graffiti.

A male graffiti writer, however, offers this more mundane explanation for the relative absence of female graffiti: "Actually most women think they're too fuckin' special to stoop to something visceral iike graffiti."

But when women do write graffiti, "the most recurring theme," according to Martilla, concerns the women's liberation movement. According to Martilla's research on the subject, approximately 25 percent of all the inscriptions found on the Berkeley campus and the surrounding community deal with this particular subject.[8]

Our own samples of female graffiti from Berkeley and other campuses throughout the country tend to be in agreement with her estimation:

> Women's john walls demand equal rights
>
> Pussy power
>
> Fill up the walls sisters! Cleaning women join us! You are the most oppressed. This room is cleaned by male cleaners.

(underneath of which was written):

> I'm pregnant—how's that for oppressed

Stocker has noted that the content and the amount of graffiti written by female students depends to an important extent on the universities they attend. At Southern Illinois University, a rather liberal institution, Stocker found that about 50 percent of the female graffiti from that campus contained a sexual theme. At the University of Missouri, which is a somewhat more conservative campus, only 26 percent of the graffiti contained any sexual content. Finally, at Western Kentucky University, the most conservative of the three, Stocker found no graffiti at all in the female restrooms, although there was no lack of such specimens in the male facilities![9]

It is probable that the women who attend the more

conservative institutions of higher learning tend to be rather conservative themselves and hence they may take a dim view of those of their sex who engage in what may be regarded as a loathsome form of masculine behavior. This in fact seems to underlie the message written by this graffiti writer to her fellow students at the University of North Carolina at Chapel Hill: "If you girls want to lead the way, don't descend to the level of men with obscene graffiti and general coarseness of language and behavior."

Speaking from her experience at the very liberal Berkeley campus, Martilla argues that "violating the taboo against defacement of property symbolizes liberation from the traditional female role of compliance. Writing latrinalia appeals to proponents of Women's Liberation because it flaunts convention and is essentially aggressive and self-assertive."[10]

When females do mark the walls, they seem to be motivated by the desire to give voice to their preoccupations rather than to find an outlet for aggression. That their themes are different from those voiced by men, such as when they touch on the women's lib movement, is to be expected, since that movement has special meaning for many women.

Likewise, when women dwell on homosexuality, it is not the male-male relationship they consider but, rather, the woman-woman one:

> Screw the man. Up with women's liberation.
> Use bananas or cucumbers or another gal for
> a good bang
>
> Girls are better than boys—you can't get
> pregnant from a girl[11]

And when women do need to release their aggression

against those whom they consider to be frustrating their ambitions, they direct their anger at the source as they see it: "Behind every bitch there is a man that fucks that bitch."

However, it is to the male anatomy, rather than the female, that some female graffitists turn for their metaphors and similes: "Life is like a penis. When it is soft you can't beat it, but when it's hard you get screwed."

Not only do women write fewer graffiti than men, but as is apparent from the few specimens that we have selected, there is very little humor present. Most female graffiti consist of bland statements. Nor did a recent article on female graffiti by Curtis Ingham in *Ms.* magazine give any examples that could be considered humorous, with the possible exception of: "A little coitus wouldn't hoitus."

Again, in the words of Lomas and Weltman, female graffiti are simply "sparse and unimaginative."[12]

NOTES

1. Lee Sechrest and Luis Flores, "Homosexuality in the Philippines and the United States: The Handwriting on the Wall," *Journal of Social Psychology*, 79 (1969), p. 11.

2. Alfred C. Kinsey, *Sexual Behavior in the Human Female* (Philadelphia: W. B. Saunders Company, 1953), p. 674.

3. Sechrest and Flores, "Homosexuality," p. 11.

4. Eugene Landy and John Steele, "Graffiti As a Function of Building Utilization," *Perceptual and Motor Skills*, 25 (1967), 711-712.

5. L. Rudin and M. Harles, "Graffiti and Building Use: The 1968 Election," *Psychological Reports,* 27 (1970), 517-518.

6. Luana Martilla, "Write On!—Goodbye to Female Compliance," in W. J. Gadpaille, "Graffiti: Its Psychodynamic Significance," *Sexual Behavior*, 2 (November 1971), p. 49.

7. Alan Dundes, "Here I Sit—A Study of American Latrinalia," *Kroeber Anthropological Society*, 34 (1966), 91-105.

8. Martilla, "Write On!" p. 49.

9. L. Stocker, "Social Analysis of Graffiti," *Journal of American Folklore*, 85 (1972), 356-366.

10. Martilla, "Write On!" p. 49.

11. R. Reisner and L. Wechsler, *Encyclopedia of Graffiti* (New York: Macmillan Publishing Company, 1974), p. 151.

12. H. D. Lomas and G. Weltman, "What the Walls Say Today: A Study of Contemporary Graffiti." Paper presented at American Psychiatric Association, New Jersey, 1966.

13 THE RISE AND FALL OF THE URBAN GRAFFITO

For all that they reveal about people and the world they inhabit, graffiti are still instances of public vandalism, although some social commentators regard graffiti as "people's art"—an attempt to beautify or improve public spaces without first obtaining official approval.

The trademarks of this folk art are its seeming anonymity, its design, and its neighborhood identity. To many, public graffiti are not acts of vandalism but legitimate expressions of the artistry of the common man. The argument is that the person who simply leaves his name or initials carved on a tree or spray-painted on a wall is a vandal. The graffiti "artist" whose work brightens a drab area and adds color to the mind-dulling blandness of the inner city, whose designs enliven the sterile concrete jungles, is considered by some to be upgrading his environment: Initials are the work of a self-centered narcissist interested only in seeing his name; but the graffiti "artist," so the argument goes, is a public benefactor.

The problem with such a distinction is that the people who must live in neighborhoods plastered with graffiti drawings are rarely polled about their interests. They are rarely consulted as to their likes and dislikes. What is art to one person may be disfigurement or vandalism to another.

Graffiti appearing on public buildings, subway cars, trees, fences, billboards, and so on, are still for the most part someone's way of leaving his mark, of letting others know that he exists. Most of the graffitists who write or draw on public buildings come from ghetto areas. They emerge from their neighborhoods individually or in gangs, spray can or felt pen in hand, ready to leave their marks throughout the city, usually in highly visible places: on buses, signposts, and so on. The goal of these spray-can gypsies is "to prove to people where I was," declares "Cool Earl," a Philadelphia graffiti writer.[1]

Recognizing that what he is doing is not approved by the establishment, the graffiti "artist" prefers to identify himself by a nickname or code name such as New York City's all pervasive Taki-183: Taki was the writer's code name, 183 his street or home address. In this way the graffitist gives himself notoriety without incriminating himself. The graffitist's code name is known to everyone on his block, and these people are his audience. They will sit in ultimate judgment of his accomplishments: "You go somewhere and get your name up there and people know you were there," explains "Cool Earl."[2]

In the slum areas of a city the prestige a graffiti writer receives from his peers is closely related to the number of times he leaves his "calling card," the hazards that had to be faced in leaving his mark in a particular place, and the style with which he portrays his name or artistry. The more perilous a locale—that is, the greater the danger of being caught or of suffering some injury—the greater the recognition given the graffitist by the peer group. In one instance, a young graffiti painter was badly burned when the sparks from a passing subway car ignited the paint he was using. Another graffitist tumbled from a train and fell to his death.

In 1972 a wave of graffiti descended on New York City's subway cars and stations. A peculiar thing happened soon after this invasion. While the transit authorities condemned the graffiti as vandalism, a segment of the city's art world began to look upon these outpourings as Radical Chic. The designs of the legendary Taki-183 and his colleagues, Hondo, Phase-Too, T-Rex 131, Me 163, began to be discussed as legitimate art.

To persuade the graffiti artists to legitimize their work formally, sociology student Hugo Martinez approached the city's gang leaders and, with their help, traced the various "writers," as the graffitists refer to themselves. Martinez persuaded them to put their work down on canvas and organized them into a registered corporation, the United Graffiti Artists (UGA).[3] Their work was subsequently displayed in New York's Razor Gallery with price tags ranging from $200 to $3,000![4] Since then some UGA members have gone on to legitimate art careers or received scholarships to study at formal art schools.[5]

The UGA also formulated its own code and social hierarchy. Established "masters" are accorded WAR status—Writers Already Respected. Their work is not to be painted over or defaced in any manner by other members. The penalty for such a violation of the graffiti writer's code is forfeiture of 30 to 50 cans of spray paint.[6]

David Bromberg, a New York City urban planner, also thought that there was more to graffiti art than vandalism. He cajoled a number of landlords into letting some graffiti artists paint murals on their buildings. Several months after these murals had been completed, they were photographed and a slide exhibit featuring these works was held at the Museum of Modern Art.[7]

Public authorities often view graffiti art in a different light than does the art community, however. In 1970 the defacement of subway stations and cars by graffiti artists cost the New York Transit Authority $250,000. In 1971 the cost was $300,000, and in 1973 it was a half-million dollars. By 1974 the cost of removing graffiti had skyrocketed to $2 million.[8]

New York City is not an isolated example of how graffiti erodes municipal budgets. In 1969 Stockholm's city council estimated that it spent approximately $36,000 a year removing graffiti from its public parks.[9] In Philadelphia the transit authorities spend $1 million annually removing graffiti in the subway system and about three times as much erasing it from the city's streets.[10]

To combat what many officials regard as a major blight New York City enacted special legislation prohibiting the carrying of opened spray cans, and about 700 persons were charged with this violation. In 1973, 1400 more were charged with the same offense. Sentences ranged from having the accused remove his own graffiti to jail sentences.[11] Some transit authority police, however, sometimes took matters into their own hands and beat up any graffiti artists unfortunate enough to be caught, before taking them in for trial.[12]

Some cities adopted alternative methods of combating the graffiti explosion. Boston erected a graffiti board in the city's Hub district around Park Street in the summer of 1971.[13] The idea was borrowed from the parks department in Stockholm, which had erected a similar board in 1969. In Boston the board is repainted every three days with quick-drying paint, and it is claimed that the project has proved so successful in cutting down defacement of public buildings that additional graffiti boards have been erected in other parts of the city. These publicly approved mediums are generally ignored by the graffiti artist, however, since they represent no challenge and are too ephemeral for his purposes.[14]

After its heyday in 1972-1973, graffiti artistry has begun to disappear. Many of the erstwhile "writers" are growing older and have begun to lose interest. Some have become discouraged by the efficiency of the city's transport workers, who are now able to remove a "masterpiece" that might have taken an entire night to produce, at great risk to the artist, less than a day after it has been created. The glory and pride in producing these paintings are simply too fleeting.

But while the artistry has begun to disappear from public graffiti, the initials, names, and code names are still very much in evidence, especially in the inner city areas of the nation's great metropolitan centers. These graffiti are not the work of "writers" but of gang members announcing that "this is our territory—stay out!" The gang name proclaims that this is the frontier —enter at your own risk:

Imperials Turf—Walk Cool

You are now entering Dragons Territory[15]

The first scientists to mention the territorial significance of graffiti, however, were Lomas and Weltman.[16] In conducting a study of the psychological significance of graffiti, they scoured the Los Angeles community, recording graffiti from the Mexican-American, black, and predominantly white residential areas of the sprawling metropolis. They found that the closer one got to the home range of a particular gang, the more graffiti one would find. But this was true only in the low socioeconomic districts. Outdoor graffiti were almost completely absent in the middle- and upper-class white neighborhoods. "By considering the cultural milieu in which the wall writer operates," says Lomas, "we find that the messages reflect shared attitudes and values as well as ethnocentric variations on main cultural themes. Thus a comparative study of contemporary graffiti is to a great extent a cross-cultural investigation of class and ethnic differences."[17] (The only cross-cultural study of graffiti is the one by Sechrest and Flores, in which they compared graffiti from the United States and the Philippines [see Chapter 8]).

More recently, the significance of graffiti as territorial markers has been the subject of an extensive report by two geographers, David Ley, of the University of British Columbia in Vancouver, Canada, and his colleague, Roman Cybriwsky, of Temple University in Philadelphia.[18] According to them, graffiti are like territorial street maps: They tell the map reader what gangs control which streets ("turf"), how tight a control they exert over their territories, which gangs are warring, and which streets are frontiers between two or more warring gangs.

The first main characteristic of gang graffiti noted by Ley and Cybriwsky, corroborates Lomas and Weltman's earlier observation that the closer one comes to the core of a gang's "turf," the more numerous the graffiti. Usually these inscriptions consist of signatures, nicknames, boastful slogans, and so on. Conversely, the farther away one moves from the core of a gang's territory, the more infrequent the graffiti written by that particular gang. Thus by paying attention to the graffiti on the various blocks, it is possible to formulate a map of the gangs in any inner-city metropolis. Graffiti can also be used to determine which gangs are fighting among themselves. This is usually indicated by the frequency of aggressive inscriptions in which taunts are hurled back and forth between gangs. Generally, these kinds of graffiti are found at contested areas between two neighboring gangs in what is sometimes referred to as a no-man's land.

The third type of inner-city graffiti designates a homogeneous defended neighborhood that is internally supportive and externally aggressive. These graffiti identify neighborhoods like South Boston, Philadelphia's Fairmount district, New York City's Harlem, and so on. Usually these graffiti take the form of racial epithets and obscenities aimed at groups that may be encroaching on the neighborhood.

Ley and Cybriwsky's unique study is one of the first of its kind to use graffiti as indicators of territoriality, gang violence, ethnic tension zones, and social attitudes among different groups. "Graffiti might be regarded, perhaps, as a rather whimsical element in the sum total of cultural baggage of interest to the social scientist," they comment, yet such inscriptions may "provide accurate indicators of local attitudes and social process in areas where more direct measurement is difficult. . . . To borrow a current graffito: 'Today's graffiti are tomorrow's headlines.' "[19]

NOTES

1. Quoted in D. Ley and R. Cybriwsky, "Urban Graffiti as Territorial Markers," *Annals of Association of American Geographers,* 64 (1974), 494.

2. Ibid.

3. S. K. Oberbeck, "Underground Artists," *Newsweek,* October 20, 1973, p. 70.

4. Ibid. For a discussion of graffiti as "People's Art" see R. Sommer, "People's Art," *Natural History,* 80 (1971), 40-45.

5. Oberbeck, "Underground Artists," p. 70.

6. Ibid.

7. Ibid.

8. *U.S. News & World Report,* June 24, 1974, p. 4; Ley and Cybriwsky, "Urban Graffiti," p. 492.

9. A. Frater, "Stick It on the Wall in Stockholm," *Holiday,* 45 (1969), 85-86.

10. Ley and Cybriwsky, "Urban Graffiti," p. 492.

11. *U.S. News & World Report,* June 24, 1974, p. 41.

12. Oberbeck, "Underground Artists," p. 70.

13. C. Bratley, "Boston's Graffiti Board," *American City,* April 1971, pp. 138-139.

14. Compare J. Hougan, "Kilroy's New Message," *Harper's Magazine,* 45 (1972), 20-25.

15. H. Kohl, *Golden Boy As Anthony Cool* (New York: Dial Press, 1972), p. 126.

16. H. D. Lomas and G. Weltman, "What the Walls Say Today." Paper presented at American Psychiatric Association, New Jersey, 1966.

17. H. D. Lomas, "Graffiti: Some Observations and Speculations," *Psychoanalytic Review,* 68 (1973), 71.

18. Ley and Cybriwsky, "Urban Graffiti."

19. Ibid., p. 491.

BIBLIOGRAPHY

American School of Classical Studies at Athens. *Graffiti in the Athenian Agora.* Princeton, N.J., 1974.

Ashbee, H. S. *Index Librorum Prohibitorum.* Privately published. London, 1877.

Bourke, J. G. *Scatologic Rites of All Nations.* Washington, D.C., W. H. Loudermilk & Co., 1891.

Brattey, C. "Boston's Graffiti Board." *American City,* 1971, pp. 138-139.

Burma, J. J. "Humor as a Technique in Race Conflict." *American Sociological Review,* 22 (1957), 107-110.

Collins, T., and Batzle, P. "Method of Increasing Graffito Responses." *Perceptual and Motor Skills,* 31 (1970), 733-734.

Comfort, A. *The Anxiety Makers.* Bristol, Thomas Nelson & Sons, Ltd., 1967.

Crawley, A. E. *The Mystic Rose.* New York, Boni and Liveright, 1927.

D'Avino, M. *The Women of Pompeii.* Naples, Loffredo Press, 1964.

Dollard, J. C., Doob, L., Miller, N., Mowere, O., and Sears, R. *Frustration and Aggression.* New Haven, Conn., Yale University Press, 1939.

Dundes, A. "Here I Sit—A Study of American Latrinalia," *Kroeber Anthropological Society,* 34 (1966), 91-105.

Dworkin, E. S., and Efran, J. S. "The Angered: Their Susceptibility to Varieties of Humor." *Journal of Personality and Social Psychology,* 6 (1967), 233-236.

Fenichel, O. "The Scoptophilic Interest and Identification."

In *Collected Papers of O. Fenichel.* New York, W. W. Norton, 1953.

Frater, A. "Stick It on the Wall in Stockholm." *Holiday,* 45 (1969), 85-86.

Freeman, R. *Graffiti.* London, Hutchinson and Co., 1966.

Freud, S. *Jokes and Their Relation to the Unconscious.* Translated by J. Strachy. London, Hogarth, 1950.

Freud, S. *Totem and Taboo.* Translated by J. Strachey. London, Routledge and Kegan Paul, 1950.

Gadpaille, W. J. "Graffiti: Its Psychodynamic Significance." *Sexual Behavior,* 2 (November 1971), 45-51.

Hartogs, R. *Four-Letter Word Games.* New York, Dell Publishing Company, 1967.

Hayakawa, S. I. *Language in Thought and Action.* New York, Harcourt, Brace and World, Inc., 1964.

Hertzler, J. O. *Laughter.* New York, Exposition Press, 1970.

History Today. The Tower of London contains on its walls an extensive collection of prisoner's graffiti, 1969, pp. 419-423.

Hollender, M. H. "The Nose and Sex." *Medical Aspects of Human Sexuality,* 6 (1972), 84-103.

Horowitz, E. L. "The Development of Attitudes Towards the Negro." *Archives of Psychology,* (1936), 194.

Humphreys, L. *Tearoom Trade.* Chicago, Aldine Publishing Co., 1970.

Ingham, C. "Graffiti. The Soapbox of the Seventies." *Ms,* 4 (1975), 65-67.

Jimenez, A. *Picardia Mexicana.* Mexico, B. Costa-Amil, 1958.

Jones, E. "Anal-erotic Character Traits." In *Papers in Psychoanalysis.* Boston, Beacon Press, 1961.

Kinsey, A. C., Pomeroy, W. B., and Martin, C. E. *Sexual Behavior in the Human Male.* Philadelphia, W. B. Saunders Co., 1948.

Kinsey, A. C., Pomeroy, W. B., Martin, C. E., and Gebhard, P. H. *Sexual Behavior in the Human Female.* Philadelphia, W. B. Saunders Co., 1953.

Kohl, H. *Golden Boy as Anthony Cool.* New York, Dial Press, 1972.

Landy, E. E., and Steele, J. M. "Graffiti As a Function of Building Utilization." *Perceptual and Motor Skills,* 25 (1967), 711-712.

Legman, G. *Rationale of the Dirty Joke.* London, Panther Books, 1969.

Ley, D., and Cybriwsky, R. "Urban Graffiti as Territorial Markers." *Annals of Association of American Geographers,* 64 (1974), 491-505.

Levine, S. "Regression in Primitive Clowning." *Psychoanalytic Quarterly,* 30 (1961), 72-83.

Lindsay, J. *The Writing on the Wall.* London, Mueller, 1960.

Lomas, H. D. "Graffiti: Some Observations and Speculations." *Psychoanalytical Review,* 68 (1973), 71-89.

Lomas, H. D., and Weltman, G. "What the Walls Say Today: A Study of Contemporary Graffiti." Paper presented at meeting of the American Psychiatric Association, Atlantic City, N.J., 1966.

Luedecke, H. E. "Grundlagen der Skatologie." *Anthropophyteia,* 7 (1907), 316-328.

Lynd, H. M. *On Shame and the Search for Identity.* New York, Harcourt, Brace and Co., 1958.

Mailer, N. "The Faith of Graffiti." *Esquire* (May 1974), 77-158.

Martial. *Epigrams.* Loeb Library.

Martilla, L. "Write on!—Goodbye to Female Compliance." In W. J. Gadpaille, "Graffiti."

Masters, W. H., and Johnson, V. E. *Human Sexual Response.* Boston, Little, Brown, and Co., 1966.

McCary, J. L. *Sexual Myths and Fallacies.* New York, Van Nostrad and Co., 1971.

Mockridge, N. *The Scrawl on the Wall.* New York, Paperback Library, 1969.

Montagu, A. *Anatomy of Swearing.* New York, Collier Books, 1967.

Myktowyca, R. "The Role of Scent Glands in Mammalian Communication." *Advances in Chemoreception.* New York, Appleton-Century-Crofts, 1970.

Oberbeck, S. K. "Underground Artists." *Newsweek,* October 20, 1973, pp. 82, 70.

Opler, M. K. "Graffiti Represent Thwarted Human Interests." In W. J. Gadpaille, "Graffiti."

Ovessey, L. *Homosexuality and Pseudohomosexuality.* New York, Science House, 1969.

Read, A. W. *Lexical Evidence from Folk Epigraphy in Western North America.* Privately published. Paris, 1935.

Reiskel, K. "Skatologische Inschriften." *Anthropophyteia,* 6 (1906), 244-246.

Reisner, R. *Graffiti: Two Thousand Years of Wall Writing.* New York, Cowles Book Co., 1971.

Reisner, R., and Wechsler, L. *Encyclopedia of Graffiti.* New York, Macmillan Publishing Company, 1974.

Reynolds, R. *Cleanliness and Godliness.* London, George Allen and Unwin, 1943.

Rhyne, L. D., and Ullmann, L. P. "Graffiti: A Nonreactive Measure." *Psychological Record,* 22 (1972), 157-168.

Rudin, L., and Harles, M. "Graffiti and Building Use: The 1968 Election." *Psychological Reports,* 27 (1970), 517-518.

Sagarin, E. *The Anatomy of Dirty Words.* New York, Paperback Library, 1969.

Schneider, R. A. "The Sense of Smell and Human Sexuality." *Medical Aspects of Human Sexuality,* 5 (1971), 157-168.

Science Digest. "Graffiti Helps Mental Patients." April 1974, pp. 47-48.

Sechrest, L., and Flores, L. "Homosexuality in the Philippines and the United States: The Handwriting on the Wall." *Journal of Social Psychology,* 79 (1969), 3-12.

Sechrest, L., and Olson, A. K. "Graffiti in Four Types of Institutions of Higher Education." *Journal of Sex Research,* 7 (1971), 62-71.

Shapiro, A. K., and Shapiro, E. "Sexuality and Gilles De La Tourette Syndrome." *Medical Aspects of Human Sexuality,* 9 (February 1975), 100-120.

Simons, G. L. *Simons' Book of World Sexual Records.* New York, Pyramid Books, 1975.

Strickland, J. F. "The Effect of Motivation Arousal on Human Preferences." *Journal of Abnormal and Social Psychology,* 59 (1959), 278-281.

Stocker, T. L., Dutcher, L. W., Hargrove, S. M., and Cook, E. A. "Social Analysis of Graffiti." *Journal of American Folklore,* 85 (1972), 356-366.

Sumner, G. *Folkways.* New York, Dover Press, 1959.

Tanzer, H. H. *The Common People of Pompei.* Baltimore, Johns Hopkins Press, 1939.

U.S. News & World Report. Subway Painting—Vandalism in the Guise of "Art." (June 1974), 41.

Webster, H. *Taboo.* Stanford, Calif., Stanford University Press, 1942.

Wolfenstein, M. *Children's Humor: A Psychological Analysis.* Glencoe, Ill., Free Press, 1954.

INDEX

About the Authors

Ernest L. Abel specializes in psychopharmacology. He has written numerous articles for such journals as *Journal of Comparative and Physiological Psychology, Psychonomic Science, Journal of Pharmacy and Pharmacology,* and *Behavioral Biology.* His previous book length works include *Ancient Views on the Origins of Life, Drugs and Behavior, The Roots of Anti-Semitism,* and *The Scientific Study of Marihuana.*

Barbara E. Buckley, Dr. Abel's wife, specializes in special education.